"WORK IS LOVE MADE VISIBLE."

KAHLIL GIBRAN

the
Business
of Bliss

How to Profit from Doing What You Love

the Business of Bliss

HOW TO PROFIT FROM DOING WHAT YOU LOVE

FROM THE EDITORS OF Victoria MAGAZINE

TEXT BY JANET ALLON

HEARST BOOKS

A Division of Sterling Publishing Co., Inc.

NEW YORK

PHOTOGRAPHED ON THE FRONT COVER:
top left, Lola Ehrlich of Lola Millinery;
top right, Kevin Simon of Kevin Simon Clothing;
bottom left, Susan Davis of Grandmother's Buttons;
bottom right, Beth Siqueland-Gresch of Grasmere

PRODUCED BY SMALLWOOD & STEWART, INC., NEW YORK CITY
EDITOR: MARIA MENECHELLA
DESIGNER: GRETCHEN MERGENTHALER
ART DIRECTOR: DEBRA SFETSIOS

Library of Congress Cataloging-in-Publication Data
Available upon request.

10 9 8 7 6 5 4 3 2 1

First Paperback Edition 2003
PUBLISHED BY HEARST BOOKS
A Division of Sterling Publishing Co., Inc.
387 Park Avenue South, New York, NY 10016

Victoria and Hearst Books are trademarks owned by
Hearst Magazines Property, Inc., in USA,
and Hearst Communications, Inc., in Canada.

www.victoriamag.com

Distributed in Canada by Sterling Publishing
ᶜ/o Canadian Manda Group, One Atlantic Avenue, Suite 105
Toronto, Ontario, Canada M6K 3E7
Distributed in Australia by Capricorn Link (Australia) Pty. Ltd.
P.O. Box 704, Windsor, NSW 2756 Australia

This book is set in Centaur

Printed in China

ISBN 1-58816-237-0

$\mathcal{T}$able of $\mathcal{C}$ontents

FOREWORD

~

For over a decade now the pages of *Victoria* magazine have been graced by the creativity of thousands of women. We began in a modest way to find women whose passions were taking them into successful business ventures. It might have seemed that one's efforts were playful—"I think I'd like to have a flower shop" or "Wouldn't it be fun to make stuffed animals?" More often than not, those notions became viable realities. The essential ingredient was always the true passion for the enterprise. It was that drive that led these women to get the support they needed and not to give up after a few wrong turns on the road to their dreams.

Because these entrepreneurs are involved in labors of love, their sharing of skills and services has been welcomed by so many others who seek goods endowed with caring. In our search to bring our readers the special, the truly one of a kind, we have met many women just like the ones you will meet on the pages of *The Business of Bliss.* Personally I have been rewarded by their stories and inspired by their hard work and their dedication to what they set out to accomplish. What is astonishing is that the well never seems to run dry. Each year more and more such stories land at our editorial offices. Always there is a new direction, even if the theme is one we've seen work in the past.

With a great deal of pride, I welcome you to this book and hope you embrace its spirit. Dream and then begin to set your plans in motion. And to all whose hearts beat with enthusiasm, we offer the examples of women, just like you, who have made the decision to fly on their own wings. If your plans are carefully made and your passion for the enterprise truly exists, then turning what you love into profit can be a blissful reality.

Nancy Lindemeyer
Founding Editor, *Victoria* Magazine

PART ONE

Inspiration

*H*ave you ever noticed how people who follow their dreams have a certain glow? Energy, confidence, and focus seem to permeate their beings.

Perhaps you've had a vague stirring, a quiet sense that there is more to life. You want to work hard at something meaningful, to share the fruits of your passion with others. You know that when you love your work, the possibilities are endless.

This book is about women of all ages and all backgrounds who dared to take a chance. Women who gathered up their resources, their childhood dreams, their particular talents, their unique vision, and poured

them into a business of their very own. What they gained was not a life free of hardship, but one of few regrets and soaring triumphs. A fuller sense of themselves, the world, and their place in it.

We think you'll find their stories inspirational.

CREATE
YOUR PASSION

Some people consider themselves artists all their lives, working daily at their craft.

Others think of "creativity" as a hobby—tinkering at home, doodling ideas on scrap

paper, making little projects to give as gifts.

These passions, hobbies, sidelines, crafts may carry the seeds of a business idea.

The response people have to your creations is the first hint: exclamations elicited when

you give a handmade gift to a friend, the inquiries of strangers about your jewelry.

Selling something you create with your own hands can be the most satisfying of

business undertakings. And there is so much out there to inspire: Nature, books,

history, legends, dreams, and everyday life give forth so much material from which

objects of beauty can be created.

Could you make these beautiful things as a full-time job? Could you make a living

doing the very thing you are compelled and happy to do?

The women in the profiles that follow decided they could.

Tailor Made

KEVIN SIMON CLOTHING

~

When Kevin Simon was a teenager she loved to draw and just assumed she'd grow up to be an artist. Since she didn't have much money and couldn't afford to buy great clothing, she made use of her creativity and simply designed her own. Her mother, a seamstress who had had her own business, helped her make these wonderful creations. Eventually Kevin's whole family started to wear her designs, and admirers would often stop them on the streets of their hometown, Buffalo, New York, to ask where they could buy similar 1920s-inspired outfits.

And so, Kevin Simon Clothing was born. In the beginning, Kevin hand-printed a catalogue of ten designs on creamy white paper and took them around to stores, many of which placed orders.

A short time later, Kevin and her whole family

picked up and moved to the greener retail pas-

tures of Venice, California, where a shop door

can stay ajar year-round. "I had to consider

myself a world-class designer, and just get out

there," said Kevin. She was all of twenty.

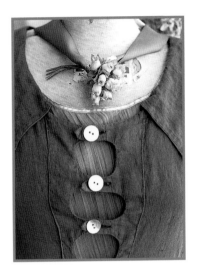

The business started on a shoestring. Upon arrival in California, her mother took a

part-time job to support Kevin while she designed her first collection and went from

store to store to elicit orders. Because they had no money, Kevin always required a deposit

up front, a practice she continues today. Through determination, long hours, and hard

work, they finally earned enough to rent a shop.

"*I get a lot back from sharing what I create.*"

The business has always been a family affair. Kevin is the head designer; her mother

sews and supervises the sewers; sister Rachel is in charge of production control and book-

keeping; brother Jeffrey minds the store; and brother Daniel is, as Kevin says, "the

problem-solver and accountant." There are advantages to having your family working with you, says Kevin. "I feel secure having them represent me when I'm not there."

That security is important, because Kevin is something of a perfectionist. She hand-dyes garments to get just the right hue, searches out the perfect vintage buttons for a dress, might bind a seam with lace, and works with only the finest natural fabrics (although she emphasizes that all of her clothes are machine-washable). She even makes her business cards by hand. "I get a

lot back from sharing what I create," she says. And as gratifying as she finds her work, it's not just about ego. Kevin had to be convinced by customers to stitch a permanent label into her garments; the result is a quirky labeling system, all her own. Sizes at the shop range from "a little

little," "a little," and "a little bigger," and her custom-made clothing bears the label "Kevin Made It My Size."

Kevin's ten-year-old business, though not huge, has been steadily growing and achieves sales from walk-in customers, mail order, and through a wholesale representative. She has expanded by designing two new lines, menswear and wedding dresses, fashion areas she finds enormously challenging and stimulating. "I've overcome wanting to be huge," she says. "I'm comfortable." But there is still one dream she covets: "I'm working towards opening a store in New York City."

Lilac Bow Yoke

Donna Allman, a trained calligrapher, loves the whimsey of illustrations from the Victorian era—black and white engravings, celestial images, children's themes. She often uses these scenes as inspiration for her business, Lilac Bow Yoke, specializing in buttons, either covered in printed cloth or protected with a glass dome, that boast these antique images. Her line also includes cabinet knobs and drawer pulls.

Kevin Simon
clothing

Creative Hands

LARK RODERIGUES
& MARY NELL'S

~

Craftwork seems to some a kind of calling, some-thing they would do whether they could make money at it or not. Their hands simply will not keep still. In quiet moments they dream up new projects. They find inspiration everywhere, and no matter how much they create, they can't wait to get into their studio to work some more. Once others start appreciating their work, and buying it, a craft that might once have been a hobby can evolve into a full-time occupation.

Both Lark Roderigues, who handpaints pottery with botanical themes in Portsmouth, Rhode Island, and Mary Anderson, a decoupage artist in

New York City, had jobs they loved: Lark worked in a topiary garden, Mary was a successful writer of children's books. Eventually, however, the demand for their craftwork began to squeeze out time from their full-time careers.

Today, even though she makes her living by creating and painting her exquisite one-of-a-kind pottery, it amuses Lark to be called an entrepreneur. "I've never thought of myself as a businessperson," she says. "I've been fortunate with my hands." To her way of thinking, she just gets up early in the morning and does what she loves all day. "I don't feel like I chose this work. I feel like it chose me."

"*I've never thought of myself as a businessperson.*"

Despite all her modesty, the fact is that Lark runs a thriving cottage industry. She is overwhelmed with orders, and since she insists on doing most of the work herself she has nearly a five-year waiting list for her dinner plates. As astonishing as that might sound, her customers seem willing to wait. "I find the wait

makes them even more determined to have it," she says. She works by appointment, and news of her creations travels by word of mouth. She also maintains a small mailing list, letting collectors know where she will be exhibiting new work. A few stores carry her pieces; one in particular, C'est La Vie in Marblehead, Massachusetts, has been a longtime supporter and promoter. "It's helpful to have a relationship with someone like that over a long period of time," she says. About four times a year she displays her wares at craft shows, stockpiling work beforehand, then suspending production to go out and meet her customers. It provides some balance with all the solitary time she spends in her studio.

Mary Anderson, who makes crafts under the name Mary Nell, also claims that creativity, not business, is her forte. Her work, decoupage plates with photos and images glued under glass, is custom-ordered for special occasions such as weddings, anniversaries, and retirements, and she works with clients' personal photos and keepsakes. Her bread and butter, however, is a wholesale line of decoupage plates that she sells through stores and catalogues and which can be produced on a large scale. "That made more sense to me," she says. "That way, the business can grow, and I can hire people for big orders." Though her company is still not at a point where she needs to hire full-time staff, she finds that for now the small scale of her business keeps her busy and fulfilled. "People's emotional reaction to the work is another kind of payment," she says.

In the beginning, Mary sold her plates at craft fairs—fun, but physically demanding work. When she was ready to shift to wholesale she discovered trade shows, in particular, the New York Gift Show, an expensive but necessary vehicle to introduce work to stores and catalogue businesses. Even then, it took a while to establish herself. "Sometimes, buyers just come around and admire your things for a year or two," she says.

With three grown daughters, grandchildren, 30 published children's books, and now her decoupage business, Mary says she is ready to share some of her writing and decoupage know-how, perhaps by teaching. "Now, I've done the two things that I always wanted to do, writing and crafts."

Your Selling Style

*I*t is one of the first decisions that faces an entrepreneur. After deciding to venture into business on your own, you must also decide how to sell your labor of love, how to reach people who will want to buy it. There are three fundamental choices available to the small businessperson: retail, mail order, and wholesale. Any of them, or a combination of them, can result in success.

Deciding whether retail is for you is largely a matter of temperament. Shop owners are by and large sociable people, who can easily chat with customers and browsers for much of the day. But opening a shop takes more than a love of people; it takes money and talent. Expenses will come from buying trips and from securing the best location, inventory, and store design. And because a store has a number of fixed costs—rent and salaries among them—it can be difficult to adapt to a changing market. Beyond the products that you carry, the design of the store, the attractiveness of the displays, and the quality of customer service are some elements that will help keep faithful customers and attract new ones. Running a shop also takes extreme dedication. Shop owners are quick to admit that running a store is like caring for a baby that needs constant care and attention.

For designers—from bridal to furniture to flower—a store is the ideal showcase. It's a chance to arrange creations exactly as you see them, to create a whole world with your vision. Some designers open a store temporarily to establish an image—a name—and then move exclusively into wholesale.

Mail order is similar to retail, although there is rarely direct contact with customers. Some mail-order businesswomen, like designers, use retail shops to showcase products and establish a large client base and extensive mailing list before turning exclusively to mail order. Other entrepreneurs try to begin directly in mail order, which may sound easy and hassle-free, but is not. Start-up costs can be quite high when you add expenses for inventory, warehouse space, printing, mailing, and shipping. Remember that mail-order businesses do not have the chance to gain customers who happen to be strolling by, which is always possible in retail, so an in-depth knowledge of the target market is crucial. This will help guide you as you determine the price of your items, decide if and when you are ready to diversify, and design a catalogue. No costs should be spared in the quality and design of the catalogue itself. This is your primary selling tool and must be unique in order to stand out from the abundance of catalogues, reach your market, and convince consumers to purchase your product.

If you have a product that can be reproduced on a large scale, and you don't wish to be tied to a shop, then a wholesale or manufacturing business may be your road to success. Remember that in wholesale the distribution of your product is what makes profit, and you must find the most efficient ways of gaining exposure for your product. Some manufacturers hire sales representatives, others place ads in trade publications, contact mail-order houses, or display at trade shows. Some even find buyers simply by taking their products around to local retail shops in their area.

Selling via the Internet is what some see as the wave of the future, and many businesswomen have begun setting up "virtual stores" to sell their products and services. Though creating a website is not cheap, start-up costs are lower than traditional retail shops, and many established businesses find websites an effective tool for reaching a larger market.

Designs from Nature

WILD CHILD

~

For Monica Schaffer, a former science teacher and a lifelong nature lover,

owning a store was a necessity born of a restless imagination. In 1992, she

was living with her three children in

the country near Wakefield, Rhode

Island, when she started making

free-form wreaths for her house. She

used wisteria vines and roots, and

sometimes thorny rosehips, creating

unexpected beauty out of what she

calls the "plainest parts of nature." Then her creations began to take over.

"My house started looking like outside. It was too much," she says. "I started taking them to other shops to sell."

After selling her designs out of other women's stores—women who became both mentors and inspirations to her—she finally, somewhat reluctantly, struck out on her own and opened a store called Wild Child. "I had about one month's worth of courage," she says,

"and about $1,000 in savings. I spent $500 on rent and I was in business before I knew it." Those first months were heady times, which Schaffer still describes with a certain childlike wonder. "My first Christmas, I didn't even have a cash register. I reached into the box where I collected the money and I couldn't believe it. There was about $2,000 in there. I had no idea what I was doing. I didn't know an invoice from a packing slip."

But she knew how to make an eye-catching arrangement, and after doing the flowers and decoration for a wedding in nearby and affluent Watch Hill, she quickly gained a well-deserved reputation for being interesting and different and not at all frilly. Clients could not get enough of her whimsical creations, some of which germinated from items she had found in road-side dumps. "People started buying things that I used as props, screen doors wrapped in vines, a rocking chair filled with flowers," she says. "They bought things I had just found in my backyard."

Divorced and with young children, Monica juggled parenting with the daily chores of running a small business, getting a friend to watch the store for a few hours in the afternoon if a child had to go to the doctor or if some other errand beckoned. What she did not know about business, she learned by doing. She visited big trade shows in New York, where she could buy cut-rate supplies. She researched tax regulations and asked fellow shop owners about hiring practices. Despite her somewhat unorthodox approach to running her business, it grew, fueled by her determination and the appreciation that others showed for her totally personal esthetic.

In addition to selling her own arrangements, Monica carried prints, notebooks, garden books, and works from local artists that she admired. Her shop's image, carefree, witty, and beautiful, slowly began to develop. "The store just evolved," she says. "It wasn't really designed." The success of the store defied expectations, and before

too long, Monica had outgrown it.

It was when she moved into the space across the street, which was five times the size of her original store, that she realized she had hit the big leagues. And with three children to raise and put through college, she knew it was time to think bigger than just having a successful little

"I had about one
month's worth of courage."

store providing a good cash flow. Now, she is ready to broaden her business with a line of clothing she has designed, which she describes as "what Cinderella would wear around the house." The future is beckoning. "I'm hoping the store will finance me into my next venture."

Fancy Footwork

VANESSA NOEL

~

As Vanessa Noel's college friends scrambled for jobs after graduation, she maintained a singular focus: she wanted to design shoes. A few years later, while carefree friends spent their summers at the beach, she was off on a trip to Milan, struggling with a rental car, a map, and a language she did not speak. She was on her way to meet and negotiate with representatives of

Italian tanneries and factories to try to begin production on her elegant shoes.

This sort of pluckiness and determination is what has enabled Vanessa to build her successful 12-year-old shoe business, with its emphasis on bridal and evening shoes. On her return from Italy and with family money behind her, she threw herself directly into the fire, opening a small store with leopard carpeting and French chandeliers off high-rent Madison Avenue, only to find that her shipment of shoes was coming in two months late from Italy. No one had told her

that the factory had closed. "I entered business naively," she admits. "But had I known everything, I might not have gone into business for myself."

Vanessa hung on, and once her shipment arrived, her high-end party shoes sold well—at least until the go-go eighties came to an abrupt halt with the recession on the cusp of the early nineties. The month of the Gulf War, "parties got canceled, people were returning shoes and dresses," she says. "I think I sold two pairs of shoes that February." She racked her brains to figure out what kind of dressy shoe people would buy even in the down times, and hit upon the idea of designing bridal shoes. "It was make or break," she says. "Either it would save us or kill us."

When she opened her all-bridal collection in the adjoining store—a collection that included white satin hiking boots—it was instantly clear that she had filled a void in the fashion market. Customers were flying in on the red-eye from Los Angeles to buy her white shoes. "Bridal is what set me apart," she says. The lesson she reiterates in speeches to would-be entrepreneurs: Don't be afraid to try.

In 1994, Vanessa opened a store in Nantucket, and published a bridal catalogue. In 1995, she launched her wholesale business, part of her business plan all along: gain exposure and a following with a retail store, then go wholesale. When she closed her New York store and rented a showroom instead, the freedom was intoxicating. "Having a store is like having a baby that's cemented to the sidewalk," she says, noting that her social life has improved since she took her business in the new direction. She is now free to pour her rather abundant energy into designing and generating ideas for her

"Having a store is like having a baby."

exquisitely feminine, yet remarkably comfortable, shoes, which are sold in upscale department stores nationwide.

For Vanessa, shoes are quirky little sculptures, and she never tires of creating them. "I still have a passion for shoes," she says. "But I think it's a healthy addiction."

What's in a Name

Like naming a child, giving a name to your company is a weighty decision. Some things to consider: The name should be memorable, and pronounceable, and should convey the nature and image of your business. Here, some examples of interesting company names and how their owners chose them:

Bell'occhio The owners of this San Francisco shop wanted a name that conveyed the store's European atmosphere and merchandise—beautiful yet useful objects from France, Italy, and Spain. They both agreed that Bell'occhio, a double entendre in Italian which can mean a good eye or an eye for the beautiful, would be perfect.

Patticakes This was Patricia Murray's pet name as a child. When she began her business making special-occasion cakes and gourmet muffins and cookies, her mother thought this would be a fitting name for her company as well. Patricia resisted at first. Now she is glad she changed her mind. Patricia admits that even when customers don't remember her name, they always remember the name of her business.

Erbe The original name of Carmen Miraglia's New York City beauty salon and natural skincare line was L'Erboristeria—"the herbal pharmacy" in Italian. Though the name revealed the essence of her company, she soon realized that it was too long and difficult for customers to remember. So she shortened the name to Erbe, "herbs," which is easy to spell and pronounce, and still expresses the Italian heritage of all her products.

Pendragon, Ink The partners of this calligraphy team wanted a name that would hark back to the Middle Ages, when the art of calligraphy was at its peak. They both loved the sound of Pendragon, which was King Arthur's father's surname (his first name was Uther). The addition of the second part of the name conjures up the image of a pen literally dragging ink across a page.

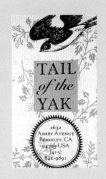

Tail of the Yak This shop carries simple luxuries, such as soap, stationery, and antique jewelry, culled from around the world. The current owners, Lauren Allard and Alice Erb, bought the store name and all. Legend has it that the original owners had asked a Tibetan monk to suggest a name for their new store. He suggested Tail of the Yak, for the yak's tail is thought to bring good fortune in Tibet. The name has served the store, which has been in business for 27 years, well.

Through the Looking Glass Trina Summins wanted her children's clothing store to appeal to both girls and boys. She hit on the universally loved Alice in Wonderland theme, which inspired the name of her shop, Through the Looking Glass, its tag line, "A Wonderland of Clothing and Gifts for Children," its color scheme (teal and yellow), and its logo, an illustration of the Cheshire Cat.

Pooter Olooms Sometimes a name with no real significance rings the right chord. This is true of Pooter Olooms Antiques, owned by Jenny Feldman. When asked what meaning the shop name holds, she admits, "It's pure nonsense. I wanted to leave open the possibility of selling absolutely anything!"

$\mathcal{T}$ogs for $\mathcal{T}$ots

BUCKINGHAM GEAR

~

The genesis of Gail Smith-Peterson's successful children's clothing store

dates from the birth of her big, bouncing baby boy. A nine-pounder at

delivery, Cody was substantial enough that by the time he was one he was

wearing outfits for three-year-olds. Dissatisfied with the clothing options

for him, Gail did a little research and found she wasn't the only mother

having trouble dressing her infant in

roomy, cute, age-appropriate clothing.

Gail, who had been a model, was also

searching for a new career that would

more easily accommodate the demands of

mothering her young son.

A self-made solution crystallized in 1992, when Gail founded Buckingham Gear, her line of European-style, high-quality, classic children's clothing. What makes her merchandise unique is a sizing system that eliminates guesswork. Items are sized by weight as well as age. "That way, you know it will fit," she reasons. "New mothers know their child's weight from frequent visits to the doctor. Even grandmothers know."

She had no real financial backing, no business experience, no schooling in design, no college education. Even her husband initially expressed doubts that she could start a business without going back to school. But Gail was determined. She began with an array of 20 adorable items, all of which she designed, cut (on her kitchen floor) and sewed. To her amazement, when she took her samples around to stores the orders poured in, and she soon had more business than she had dared to dream of.

Three years later, the Buckingham Gear line had expanded to more than 50 items of clothing, and Gail was also offering children's bathwear and accessories. She went from strictly wholesale to retail when she opened a small boutique in Encinitas, California, north of San Diego, decorated it with vintage furniture, and named it Buckingham Mercantile. Her store, like her label, bears the mascot of a delightful moose named Buckingham.

"If someone does it all for you, you don't learn how to run a business."

It's been a lot of hard work, but Gail says she's glad she started small, grew slowly, and declined offers of partnerships so that she could learn from trial and error. "If someone does it all for you, you don't learn how to run a business," she says. "I know it will take me longer to get there, but when you have passion for what you do, that will get you through."

The Finer Things

BRAVURA

~

Bravura, an opera term meaning "a spirited execution," was originally supposed to be the name for Denise Fiedler's business of importing Italian fabrics. But when Denise found she couldn't make a living as an importer, she pulled out her trusty sewing machine and began making sachets stuffed with lavender and cedar from the linens she had stockpiled. She took them around to neighboring San Francisco stores and when they quickly sold out, she knew she had a viable business. Bravura, she decided, would fill the niche in the market for sachets and other feminine accessories that weren't too "frou-frou," she says. "They wouldn't just be pink and lace, pastel and white. It all started to click."

Not that the tough times were behind her. She had one particularly panicky moment when she received a big order from a department store and had no cash to buy the supplies to fill it. Too small to get a loan from a bank,

"You always need to be looking for inspiration."

she borrowed $5,000 from friends. It took two years for her to earn a living at what had once been her hobby, handcrafting her lingerie bags, purses, and pillows, adorned with brocades, ribbons, and tassels.

Slowly, her business grew and with it, her cash flow. It wasn't long before she had to hire staff to help her fulfill all the orders. "That

was hard," she says. "It forced me to take my business seriously. Hiring people was symbolic of the shift from this being my hobby to making it a business."

With her products in nearly 250 stores across the country, the lessons in how to run a business keep coming. Lessons like ordering supplies well in advance, having back-up suppliers, and pricing her work so that every-thing—materials, time, and even last-minute shipping—are taken into account. "Everyone has a different formula," she says. "I find it's best to add a five or ten percent fudge factor," which is used to cover any unanticipated costs.

Nearly ten years after starting Bravura, the hardest part of her business now, says Denise, is generating new ideas quickly enough for today's fast-moving marketplace. "You always need to be looking for inspiration, which can be found anywhere," she says, "during a walk to work, from a leaf on the ground, from travel, or reading." Despite the pressure to always be creative and the stress often associated with running her own busi-ness, she finds the ability to make her own decisions, in her career and life, empowering.

$\mathcal{P}$ersonal $\mathcal{A}$rt

WELLS-WARE

~

The idea came to Wells Jenkins, a young archi-

tect in New York City, overnight. As she slept,

Wells dreamed of a necklace filled with mean-

ingful charms made up of family photographs,

old postcards, lace, and keepsakes from her

childhood, all miniaturized and mounted in

tiny silver frames. Although Wells had never created jewelry, she had always

made things with her hands, and the next day she set about making her dream

necklace. "I figured if I can make a building, I can make a piece of jewelry,"

she says. For the next two weeks, she wore her family photo necklace every-

where, and it drew so many comments that she knew she was on to something.

When she showed it to the jewelry purchasers for a large department store and they immediately ordered 50, she called up some friends and said, "We've got work to do."

That was when Wells-Ware, a line of jewelry as personal as one individual's memories, was born. Since then, Wells has been extremely busy creating—designing and making jewelry (necklaces, cufflinks, earrings, bracelets) and Christmas tree ornaments, ready-made as well as made-to-order. She has built up a mailing list, given sample sales, appeared on "The Oprah Winfrey Show" in segments about ideal Mother's

"*I can't wait to get out of bed in the morning . . . .*"

Day gifts and "What To Do With Your Baby Photos," and learned the ropes of running her own small business. "I work harder than I ever did when I was an architect," she says, without a trace of complaint in her voice. "But now, it's for myself."

Wells works from photos supplied by the customer, reducing them to tiny black-and-white or sepia shots to make them look antique. Her customers can also avail themselves of items in her eclectic collection, which includes charms, bows, hearts, mother-of-pearl buttons, antique watch faces, and old photographs rescued from estate sales. Wells has located her studio, itself a quirky archive of a lifetime of tasteful

collecting, in the building where she grew up. Her mother, her right-hand person and one of her full-time employees, scrupulously maintains the Wells-Ware mailing list of 10,000 and helps with public relations events.

Though busiest around holidays like Christmas and Valentine's Day, Wells-Ware also takes many orders throughout the year. "I've made bracelets with snippets of a bride's gown or pressed flowers from her bouquet, and many necklaces for new parents—with baby pictures, photos of footprints, birth announcements.

"I love making things that mean something to people," Wells says. "And pictures mean so much to people at any age." Most fulfilling to her is the huge amount of mail she receives from grateful, deeply moved clients. "I love what I do. I can't wait to get out of bed in the morning to do it."

A Romantic

LOUISE GREEN

~

Styles may come and go, but hats, award-winning milliner Louise Green has discovered, have an eternal appeal. Certainly her romantic, vintage-inspired, thoroughly modern, beautifully detailed hats, which she began making more than ten years ago, do.

British-born, Louise says she always wore hats as a child and loved the way they added color and richness to London's streets. After studying fine art in Brighton, England, she moved to Los Angeles in 1983, when vintage clothing was the rage. Louise, who had two small children, was looking for a way to earn some money. First she bought a vintage tuxedo jacket, decorated it, and sold it on consignment in a gallery. It sold, but only after a while. But a hat she bought and retrimmed sold right away. That was the birth of her business.

She signed up for millinery classes, discovering that the art of hatmaking was being kept alive primarily by African-American church-going women. She learned all she could from these teachers, and then cautiously began her own business, making hats in her living room. She was still uncertain whether producing an item that many people love, yet few people actually need, was viable as a business. But when she took her wares around to Los Angeles's finest stores, the response was very positive. Soon her husband, an architect, joined her to help run the business. About 1,000 stores across the country, including Saks, Neiman Marcus, and Nordstrom, now carry her hats—

which are manufactured in a 6,000-square-foot facility with a staff of 15 in West Los Angeles.

The success of her business has defied the odds, but Louise concedes that it has not always been easy, especially as most women don't wear hats on a regular basis. Louise feels that her success is in large part due to her passion, and her ability to pass that passion on to her customers. "I was one of those people who always knew I was talented at something," she says. "I'm very true to the vision that I have, which is to make soft, romantic hats."

Working at Home

*M*any small businesses begin at home. With sufficient space and understanding roommates or families, a house can be transformed into a beehive of industry. Working at home keeps overhead low, and is often an ideal solution when you are first starting out and have little capital. You can always rent a space as your business expands and more space is needed.

Some things to consider before setting up a home office: Do local zoning laws allow you to operate a business from a private residence? Is it necessary to apply for permits, licenses, or extra insurance coverage? Will clients need to come to your home office, and if so, will they consider it professional?

For businesswomen with children, working at home is often the ideal situation. Elizabeth Terry, chef and proprietor of Savannah's Elizabeth on 37th, opened her lavish restaurant only after she and her husband bought a historic mansion and needed to find a way to use the space besides living in it. Perhaps the biggest bonus of having combined her business and residence, says Elizabeth, is that she was able to spend time with her two daughters while they were growing up, and simultaneously pursue her career as a groundbreaking chef.

But all work-at-home entrepreneurs agree that it is imperative to learn how to separate business and home life. Designate a specific work area to minimize family interruptions, and set up specific company hours so that clients are not calling you during "family" time. Rachel Ashwell, a mother and the founder of Shabby Chic, found it helpful to designate one staff member from her office to relay all messages to her when she was working at home.

At First Glance

As every successful retailer knows, a good sign is crucial to a good first impression. Match the sign to your business: A simple wooden placard hanging over the entrance might suggest an unpretentious shop with a country air, while a fancy Victorian scroll painted on a shop window boasts more ornate merchandise. Whatever visual ideas you may have for your sign, it is always good to consider hiring a graphic illustrator who is sensitive to the image you are trying to create. Other elements to keep in mind are whether your customers will be driving or strolling by, and if illumination would help attract evening business.

At Your Service

Your aim is to please clients, to make for them the perfect meal, the tastiest dessert, the lushest garden. You want to offer a complete experience that engages all the senses, at least for a time. Your creativity has led you into a service-oriented business, with all of the gratification that comes from helping and delighting people.

Being successful in a service industry means more than making an object and selling it. Of course, even the service industry is part science, part art. If you are looking to start a restaurant, you already know that your job is not just simply to create wonderful dishes; you must also set a mood—with your decor, your staff, your lighting. A garden designer must not only be an expert in plants but also a visionary who can create an Eden. As the provider of a service, you must, above all, be able to sense your customers' taste, anticipate what they want, and adapt your vision accordingly.

For your know-how, and your taste and vision, there are plenty of potential clients, and plenty of rewards if you plan your business well.

Tasty Little Bite

BONNE BOUCHE

~

Karen Aulbach and Aimee Murphy met while working in a restaurant near San Jose, California, became friends, and soon realized they shared a dream: to start their own business. The women certainly had complementary talents. Karen is a chef committed to cooking with the best, freshest food. Aimee loves to set tables, develop visual themes, bring an aura to an event. "I love food," says Aimee, "but I have no desire to get in the kitchen and cook."

The two women considered opening a restaurant, but eventually opted for a catering business. There were distinct advantages: less risk, lower start-up costs, and the opportunity to let their creativity soar. After catering several parties, their reputation grew and their business took off.

Karen and Aimee named their business Bonne Bouche, French for "tasty

mouthful" and "tasteful palate." Based on the Monterey Peninsula, they cater occasions large and small: weddings, corporate parties, baby showers, and as many charitable functions as possible, both for publicity and because they want to give back to the community.

The two friends both have a knack for service, for taking the vague notions of a client and transforming them into a wonderful and memorable event. Brides are especially grateful. "People think they know what they want for a wedding, but all they really know is they want everything to be perfect," says Aimee. Bonne Bouche makes the dream of perfection concrete, and includes nervous clients in the process. The partners bring sample table settings and menus to initial meetings with clients to glean feedback and suggestions, though they find many party givers are content to hand over all the decisions to the tasteful caterers.

"Every event is totally different," says Karen. "We have catered everything from luaus and clambakes on the beach to elegant dinner parties with only four guests." Though they both came to catering with an intrinsic understanding of food, neither woman had much business experience. They have learned by doing, making a few mistakes, and moving on. Starting out required an investment of about $10,000, says Aimee, which they

"Don't wait for someone to knock on your door with an opportunity."

got from investors. Despite their inexperience, they knew enough to carefully document all the terms. "California is a very litigious state!" says Aimee.

Hard work though it is—"You never really get a break," says Aimee—the two

women are having the time of their lives. Karen's advice to other aspiring entrepreneurs: "Just do it. If you have a vision, don't hold back. Don't wait for someone to knock on your door with an opportunity. Just go out and do it."

Garden Designs

CONNI CROSS

~

The evolution of Conni Cross's garden design and installation business has been as long and winding as adulthood itself, following an internal logic and flowing in and out of the significant personal events of her life. What is now a bustling enterprise on Long Island's North Fork began simply enough and out of the necessity that often mothers invention. "I started out as a young woman with an art background needing to make some money," says Conni.

A deep bond with an older woman who owned a large local peach farm provided Conni with much of her love and knowledge about plants. Her

first foray into business was when she purchased as many hanging baskets as $150
would buy from a local greenhouse, then
threw what she dubbed a "houseplant party"
at her house, much in the tradition of the
Tupperware parties that were fashionable at
the time. She sold every one of the plants

*"I started out as a young woman
. . . needing to make some money."*

and received orders for more. Conni continued to host plant parties while she

concentrated on making a name for herself and expanding her contacts. Blessed with a

green thumb as well as a

creative eye, she soon start-

ed planting tropical plants

in containers and selling

those. Eventually, she was

hired to design a garden in

someone's home. "That's what led to the landscaping business," she says, recounting the birth of her garden and landscape design firm.

Soon after Conni's first venture into garden design, she married Jim Cross, who ran a local plant nursery she had begun to frequent. Together they built a house, had a child, gardened, and coached other gardeners. They ran their separate businesses side by side until Jim's death a few years ago. The house they built and the garden they installed there became a showcase for Conni's living sculpture. "Unlike other designers, we don't do plans," says Conni. "We show clients how gardens develop by using showcase homes."

One of the trickiest parts of Conni's enterprise is the juggling it entails. "Maintenance has become a large part of the business," she says. "I'm thinking of making it a division of the company and paying people more to just do that." She solved the problem of finding herself on the phone every night until 11 p.m. by getting a cellular phone, so she can return calls from her car. "It's expensive but a good investment," she says. To reduce the cost of her in-house communications, she bought walkie-talkies.

Now a grandmother, Conni shows no signs of slowing down. And plants have become the family business across generations. Her daughter, Jessica, who grew up surrounded by Conni's lush plantings and inspirational gardens, now runs the nursery.

Pricing Your Work

You have made something beautiful that you have doted on every minute of its creation. Now comes the strange part: deciding how much to charge for your beautiful something. For many artists/designers turned entrepreneurs, quantifying their labors in dollars and cents is extremely tricky business. Women, in particular, have a tendency to undervalue the things that they make, to discount their own time and energy in the pricing equation. This inclination to sell yourself and your products short is one of the first obstacles you'll need to overcome when you make a business out of your bliss. Though you may be doing what you love, you must consider what you do a business, and treat it as such.

The first piece of advice that successful women entrepreneurs give is to keep scrupulous written records. You must know your costs for everything—rent, advertising and publicity, employee salaries, materials, shipping, packaging, buying trips, and so on. And remember to charge a fee for your own labor, which should include not just the time taken to create your product or provide your service, but the time spent buying supplies, selling, meeting with prospective investors, and performing administrative and bookkeeping tasks.

Once you have determined your total costs, you will be able to establish your break-even point—the amount of money you will need to charge to cover all of these expenses. Then you should shop around and determine what your competition is charging for similar products or services. Depending on the uniqueness of your product or service, you may want to charge a little more or less.

With your break-even point in mind, and a sense of how much you will charge for your own time, you must determine your profit ratio. Although formulas vary for the mark-up—depending on whether you work in retail, wholesale, or a service industry—the general rule is a 20 percent add-on for profit.

Always bear in mind, however, that costs and prices fluctuate, and that sometimes the best way to attract and keep customers is by making them feel that you are taking care of them and are willing to give them a break on occasion. "If I get a good price on something, I'll pass

it on," says Marlene Harris, an antiques dealer. "I love a great bargain, and so do you." Customers of any income level want to feel that they are getting a good value. "We always try to be fair, but make a profit," says Joyce Eddy, founder and CEO of the furniture company Habersham Plantation. Her advice: "Keep the prices as low as possible while maintaining high quality."

Sweet Tooth

PINK ROSE PASTRY SHOP

~

Julie Van de Graaf had only recently graduated from college, with a degree in art and an apprenticeship in French pastry, when she started baking and selling delectable individual pastries from her home in Philadelphia to local stores and restaurants. The response was always positive, and as sales grew more brisk, Julie, possessed of an optimistic temperament, took a plunge that she now chalks up to youthful enthusiasm and naivete. She decided to give up her job in a restaurant and wholesale her pastries full-time.

Before long, she realized she needed a larger space and larger ovens than what she had at home and, equipped with a $12,000 loan from her father, she rented a space in Philadelphia's wholesale food district. The Pink Rose soon became known as a diamond in the rough in South Philadelphia.

Not only did the shop boast some of the most delicious sweets in town, but it was home to one of the few cappuccino and espresso makers as well. The pastries drew people into the shop, but being able to get a

"...This has been my master's education in business."

frothy cup of cappuccino at just about any time of day was a bonus customers seldom failed to appreciate. When coffee bars opened in droves several years ago, Julie's retail business felt the pinch. Her solution: "We started selling pastries to the coffee bars wholesale," says Julie. "When you get lemons, you make lemonade."

The over-arching lesson that she took from the experience was the importance of diversification, even in a highly niched service industry like a pastry shop. Julie has diversified in another way, by developing a once-a-year holiday mail-order business. She had repaid her father's start-up loan by sending all of his clients Christmas cookie tins, thus developing a loyal following that faithfully order cookies for themselves and their friends during the holidays.

Market forces also redirected Julie's business when a new landlord offered an unap-

pealing short-term lease on the space she had been renting. It spurred Julie to search for another locale, which she found between Philadelphia's tony Society Hill and touristy South Street with its thriving street scene. The appealing shop now generates much of its business from walk-in customers strolling by, who immediately take to Julie's obvious delight in catering to them.

Not a born businesswoman, Julie admits that the business lessons have come less naturally than her baking skills. To close the gap, she has taken some business courses and tries to surround herself with people who are strong where she is weak. "You learn by doing it," she says. "My father says this has been my master's education in business."

Urban Dreams

POTTED GARDENS

~

Sometimes an idea for a business grows as naturally as an unweeded garden during a damp New England summer. This is more or less what happened for Rebecca Cole, a self-described "country girl" who moved to New York City to pursue a career in acting, and ended up starting a lucrative business creating and designing container gardens for city folk instead.

Like most aspiring actors, Rebecca had to work other jobs, such as bartending, to get by. More fulfilling was a stint as an AIDS activist, but this, too, eventually became frustrating. Rebecca has always been a free spirit and suspected she'd be better off working for herself. Her refuge was the garden she planted on her small terrace, a reminder of idyllic summers in New Hampshire, and of her grandfather, who taught her everything she

knows about plants and gardening. During those summers, she says, "I fell in love with natural-looking spaces and old junk."

Many of Rebecca's friends admired her garden in the city, and asked for her help in designing their own. When friends of friends began making the same request, Rebecca realized she had a viable business venture, and started to charge money for her services. While gardening was the one thing that made her truly happy, she did not want to be merely other people's hired hand, so she

"I needed a way to show off my style."

formulated a business plan. "I needed a way to show off my style," she says. "All I could think of was opening a store." For that she needed money, so she struck a deal with a wealthy client, who agreed to loan her $5,000 over five years. Rebecca was to pay off the interest immediately by designing a spectacular garden for her.

Rebecca's six-year-old business, Potted Gardens, has doubled every year since then. Her store in bustling Greenwich Village displays an appealing array of plants, flowers, garden antiques, and botanical art. But there is more to her business than meets the delighted eye. She offers garden design, floral design for weddings and other events, sells antiques and flowers retail, and recently wrote a book, *Potted Gardens,* that lays out her vision for bringing the wild and colorful palette of a country garden to plant-starved urban dwellers. What makes Rebecca's designs unique is not just her knowledge of plants, but her use of unusual and unexpected containers for them, from old cigar boxes and antique cookie tins to sap buckets, suitcases, and wooden toy trucks—"anything, in fact, that will hold soil," she says.

Running the business is an engaging but hectic life, so hectic in fact that Rebecca

 has promised herself to consolidate. "I wouldn't recommend doing three things at the same time," she says. Her somewhat tongue-in-cheek advice: "Be careful, you might succeed."

Choosing Staff

If you're fortunate and your business grows to the point that you can no longer handle the workload alone, you will face a challenge shared by every business, large and small—finding good help. Business owners all agree: Making good hires is one of the hardest and most important aspects of any job. How do you find people who will tend to your business responsibly, and serve your customers the way you want them to? Here, businesswomen offer some tips on hiring borne from experience.

"Look for people who want to start a business like yours in three years, who want to learn everything about it. Don't be threatened by that."

Rebecca Cole, *Potted Gardens*

"Once you have staff people you like, pay them a little more than the competition. Turnover is painful, retraining time-consuming. In a small business, relationships with customers and continuity are very important."

Joan Gers and Cynthia Conigliaro, *Archivia*

"Be a good delegator. Let people do what they were hired to do."

Rachel Ashwell, *Shabby Chic*

"Hire the best and cry once. You might have to pay them a lot, but the job will get done."

Joyce Eddy, *Habersham Plantation*

"Be open and honest with your employees. Pay well. Don't expect people to work over 45 hours a week, even in the restaurant business, but expect them to work hard when they are there. It takes flexibility and teamwork."

Elizabeth Terry, *Elizabeth on 37th*

"Always hire people who are smarter than you are."

Patti Upton, *Aromatique*

"The most important thing is to have a group of people who get along together. A small business has to be a family-type atmosphere."

Louise Green, *Louise Green Millinery*

"Surround yourself with people who are passionate about what they do."

Susan Kelly Panian, *Whispering Pines*

"Provide a stable environment and try to let people do what they are good at. I encourage my staff to go to exhibitions and lectures and to join junior committees for charities. And I always give off for Thanksgiving, a week in August, and a week between Christmas and New Year's. You can't be fresh at work without some joy at home."

Charlotte Moss, *Charlotte Moss & Company*

"Don't be too hasty to hire. Stay small. Don't promise what you can't deliver. Take it one step at a time."

Karen Skelton, *Potluck Studios*

"Hiring mistakes are best dealt with early. You know right away if it's not going to work. If it isn't, you need to nip it in the bud."

Yolanda Tisdale, *Yesteryear*

"Create a scenario that employees can live with. This goes beyond good benefits. We allow people to create their own schedules, give two weeks off at Christmas, and sometimes hold business meetings in the pasture. For all of us, it's a total journey."

Tracy Porter, *Tracy Porter: The Home Collection*

"Hire happy people."

Nancy Clark, *Old Chatham*
Sheepherding Company and Inn

Framing a Vision

YESTERYEAR

~

Yolanda Tisdale's eye for antiques was culti-vated from an early age, and she continued to collect prints and other unique items even as she pursued a career in television producing in Los Angeles. One day, an opportunity in the antiques field presented itself, one that she could not refuse. A friend with a well-established business selling prints in a great location on tony Melrose Avenue was retiring. Yolanda decided that inheriting the nuts and bolts of a shop was easier than starting from scratch, and she took the plunge. Her shop, Yesteryear, sells antique prints and specializes in a rare and original approach to custom-framing, using tartans, damask, tweeds, ribbons, and brocades. "The

frame gives the art a whole different dimen-

sion," she says.

One of the biggest challenges of her

business, says Yolanda, is educating her clients

and encouraging them to view things, as she

does, with a fresh eye. "You can take some-

thing very modern and work it into an antique setting," she says. And Yolanda is a

master at envisioning just what her clients want. Yesteryear has framed heirloom

wedding dresses, baby shoes, and pocket watches, imbuing each object with new life.

"I tell people . . . that they'll never look at framing the same again."

Yolanda bought the business with a longtime friend, interior designer David Harte,

with whom she shared taste and vision, and the partners used their personal savings as

their initial start-up capital. David's contacts in the interior design industry, the store's

location across the street from the Pacific Design Center, and the owners' energetic pro-

motion at interior design trade shows built visibility and allowed Yesteryear to develop

an important working relationship with the Los Angeles interior design community.

But it is Yolanda who runs the business day to day, handling the process of hiring and training framers who are not just performing a job but practicing a trade. She describes the store as a salon/atelier, where patrons are invited to linger on sofas and skilled craftspeople patiently assemble perfect frames.

She has learned that she needs employees who share some of her passion, and that

"It just never occurred to me that I couldn't do it."

her business runs best when everyone gets along. It helps that she is a woman brimming with confidence. "There are pitfalls in any business," she says. "It just never occurred to me that I couldn't do it."

Showing Off

For artisans and artists who create one-of-a-kind pieces, craft shows provide a wonderful opportunity to meet their public, especially for those just starting out. For businesswomen who are making products on a larger scale and are able to fill big orders, the most efficient way to reach potential customers is through trade shows. Every industry—from gourmet foods and antiques to giftwares—has an annual trade show in major cities, such as the well-attended New York Gift Show. But there are also many regional shows at local convention centers, which are an excellent way to become familiar with the trade show experience and make contacts with local businesses. Participation in a trade show, especially a large one, is expensive—on average $3,000 for the smallest space, and this does not include travel expenses, hiring of staff, installation of your display, and printing of promotional material—but it is often the only way small businesses can gain access to people with important positions at key companies. Remember, buyers from the smallest independent shops to the largest major department stores attend these shows searching for new merchandise.

Always attend a trade show before you decide to set up a booth. This allows you to learn about your market and assess the competition you will face. It is also a wonderful way to get ideas for your displays, and to meet suppliers who may provide you with a something necessary to your own product or service: pretty boxes for your hats, wonderful bottles for your bath oils. Be sure to keep a list of names and companies that interest you. And hold on to the show directory, which lists all the participating companies and products displayed. This can be an invaluable resource and research tool.

Southern Charm

ELIZABETH ON 37TH

~

Never mind the accolades and honors that have been bestowed over the years on Elizabeth Terry and her Savannah restaurant, Elizabeth on 37th. What really gratifies this celebrated chef is that she was able to be a hands-on mother to her daughters, Alexis and Celeste, and pursue a sterling career at the same time. She did this by raising her family in the same turn-of-the-century mansion in which her famous restaurant is located. "It's been very rewarding," she says. "Our kids were not latchkey kids. When they had friends over, they brought pretty dresses and came down to the restaurant."

Elizabeth had always cooked with what she calls a "mad passion."

Her first foray into the food business was in Atlanta, where she opened a small sandwich shop. When she and her husband, a successful lawyer, moved their family to Savannah in 1980 in search of a slower pace of

life, she thought she might just open another sandwich shop. That was until they found

the house where they thought their destiny resided, a Greek revival villa with huge Palladian

"*I was always the boss. I highly recommend that.*"

windows and urns atop its roof in Savannah's eccentric, historic neighborhood. The build-

ing is massive, says Elizabeth, and it was only when they were brainstorming on how to fill

it up that they hit upon the idea of opening a restaurant.

Husband Michael decided to take a year off from law to help launch the restaurant and serve as its wine steward,

where his knowledge of the restaurant's
extensive wine list never fails to impress
diners. That was almost 20 years ago, and
he has never gone back to practicing law.

Reviews of the 75-seat restaurant, which is divided into four comfortable rooms and
offers first-rate service in an elegant setting, have been uniformly positive. Elizabeth serves
a unique yet familiar brand of Southern food, including lots of seafood from the coastal
waters nearby. Dishes like softshell crabs with corn succotash and chicken crusted with
almonds and cream rice are perennial favorites. Tourists and locals flock to the restaurant,

and Elizabeth has gradually broken into the
male-dominated echelon of the country's top
chefs, twice being honored by the prestigious
James Beard Foundation.

Meanwhile, Savannah's profile has risen,
in large part because of the Savannah-set
bestseller, *Midnight in the Garden of Good and Evil*
by John Berendt, which featured Elizabeth on

37th. Elizabeth too has expanded her horizons beyond running her restaurant and has recently set down some of her own recipes and colorful memories of Savannah in her book, *Savannah Seasons: Food and Stories from Elizabeth on 37th.*

A reluctant trailblazer, Elizabeth's success arises from a simple love of cooking and a willingness to follow her instincts. Of course, she also worked her share of long hours, and sometimes, she jokes, exploited child labor by enlisting her daughters to help shell peas. Looking back, though, things have gone much the way she would have wanted them to go. "I was always the boss," she says. "I highly recommend that."

Nancy's Wines

It was Nancy Maniscalco's passion for food and wine that inspired her to open her own store in New York City. Nancy's Wines for Food is committed to teaching people about the best combinations of food and drink. Her shop is user-friendly, and features wall charts that provide customers with hand-written recipes and menu suggestions for each vintage. Nancy is always available to offer advice, and often hosts informal wine tastings.

POUPI LA POUPEE

OBJECTS D'ART PAR DENISE LANDRIAULT

The Dish
ran away with
the spoon, inc.

housewares
&
cool stuff

510 Commercial
Anacortes, WA 98
(360) 293-136

Calling Cards

The design of a calling or business card should be one of your first considerations once you have chosen a name for your company. Unusual business cards are always the most memorable, so consult with a designer and consider odd shapes, bright colors, or interesting patterns. It is a good idea to carry a stack with you at all times. You never know where or when you will meet someone who is interested in what you sell.

Mme. Hollyhock

Celebrate With Flowers
memorable weddings,
occasions, & events

Flowers custom designed

Kim Miller 784-1292
Patricia Grazini 367-8207

Seattle, WA

Annlimited

The Sisters

OPEN STUDIO
30 Kenwood Street
in
Brookline
232-3583

Lots of warm wools and
a linen preview for Spring...
Stop in to sip tea and try on a hat or two!
Saturday and Sunday, January 30 and 31, 11-6 noon-6p

Lindsey Shaw
Catering
(416) 926-9133

The Johnston House

Antiques & Interiors
RD #4 Route 228 • Mars, Pennsylvania 16046
(412) 625-2636

B A R T L E T T

Maine Estate Winery
Premium fruit wines of Maine

Robert Bartlett

THE ENGLISH ROOM

FINDING
A NICHE

You have an ability to spot the gems among the dust. You can roam through flea

markets and estate sales and emerge with the prizes. Your creativity resides in your

ability to discover beauty in overlooked, unappreciated things, to arrange those hidden

treasures in a startlingly new way that renders their beauty apparent.

Or you have always had a passion for antiques, for a particular era, for Limoges,

for lace. And you have taken care to educate yourself about them over the years. You

could surround yourself with such objects and talk to others who share your enthusi-

asm all day, and count the days spent as among the best in your life. You could start a

business buying and selling these objects of your affection. Perhaps you already have a

collection that is filling your home to overflowing, and that could form the core of your

own company devoted to spreading the word about your own passion.

The women in these profiles turned their passion for a particular item into smart

business ideas, and it was the best decision they ever made.

Collecting Rarities

ARCHIVIA BOOKS

~

Joan Gers and Cynthia Conigliaro had reached a point in life where they did

not want to work for anyone else. Both had careers in the book business, and

they had developed a friendship and mutual respect trading tips on where to

get the best decorative art and architecture titles. Both had tired of
working long days to make money
for someone else. Cynthia wanted to
have a baby, and wanted the flexible
hours that her own business would
allow. Both women wanted to have a
store where they called the shots.

To walk into their elegantly designed, 450-square-foot Madison Avenue store called Archivia is to get lost in a world of beautiful books. Here, the two women have created a successful business amassing an inventory of out-of-print, foreign, and rare titles on just three topics: architecture, interior design, and gardens. In a time when megastores dominate the book business, Archivia is managing, after seven years in business, to turn a small profit. "We're in a solid position now," says Cynthia. "Now, we can expand."

In the beginning there were cash crunches, hiring mistakes, and long hours. "You have to make up your mind to go for it," says Joan. "We never had to speak about how we both have tenacity. It was just assumed. It never occurred to us to close."

The two partners are so like-minded that they finish, and sometimes start, each other's sentences. "Whenever there's a problem, we sit down and figure it out," says Cynthia. Their skills are also complementary. Joan deals with customers, spending time to figure out what they need. "Our customers are very familiar to us," they both agree.

"We know their taste. If customers do not have a specific book in mind, we show them

ten books they never considered." Cynthia, for her part, deals with administrative work,

stays on top of the finances, and designs and writes the store's catalogue. Her degree in

architecture helps her maintain and cultivate the store's professional clientele—architects,

designers, and museum curators—a significant part of their success. Their staff of six is

"You have to make up
your mind to go for it."

carefully chosen, and employees are paid better than at most bookstores to avoid frequent

turnover. Apart from walk-in traffic generated from the area's many museums, Archivia

boasts a mailing list of 11,000, which the owners have built from the ground up.

Archivia has the feel of a library, where

one can do serious research into highly special-

ized subjects—Scottish houses, French

antiques, Roman gardens. This small shop has

won awards for its store design, where dark

green walls and dark stained floors reveal an

approach to books that is cerebral yet inviting.

Something Old

CORNELIA POWELL

~

For Cornelia Powell, who was raised on a farm in Alabama and spent four years as a magazine editor in New York, fabrics have always held a nearly spiritual power. Cornelia can trace this back to her childhood and her grandmother, at whose knee she would sit as a girl, listening to tales of parties and party dresses, ribbons, bows, and perfect curtsies. "It was poetry to me," says Cornelia. "Her stories conjured up a whole world."

When she left New York and headed back south to Atlanta, Cornelia knew she eventually wanted to open her own small shop, one that would involve dressing women. Working as a freelance wardrobe consultant, she forged a partnership with a local 18th- and 19th-century lace wholesaler with whom she sometimes did "trunk shows." These limited-viewing fashion shows (called trunk shows because the merchandise was literally packed in trunks). It was a transforming experience, and one that helped Cornelia establish a substantial following. "I loved what happened to me when I worked with these textiles," she said. "It connected me to something deep and mystical." It was after Diana and Charles's royal wedding in 1981 that Cornelia had a vision for a store. She realized that

people would never look at weddings the same: "After that wedding, romance was fashionable again. Weddings were chic." In her new career, she decided she would carry vintage laces and cater to brides, though not exclusively.

Cornelia had little start-up capital, but she felt she was ready to go and opened her shop in 1986. She kept overhead costs as manageable as possible by finding a low-rent space on the second floor of a busy shopping street, and carrying items on consignment. Soon brides of all ages flocked to her. It was the lace that lured them, the fairyland quality of the store, as well as the designers and tailors Cornelia hired, geniuses at the art of recycling vintage textiles and creating the perfect fit. Cornelia also offered something more, a chance for a woman to express her personality through her wedding dress. Here, dressing was truly an art form.

The success of the little shop meant that the time came to expand to the larger, more visible storefront below, and for all of her confidence in her creative abilities, Cornelia was terrified. To afford the larger space, she would need to triple her sales and hire more staff. "I felt so vulnerable and exposed," she

"I wanted to take my message to a bigger arena."

says. "If it didn't work, everyone would know." She decided to trust her instincts, something she had always advised her clients to do when selecting a dress. Her instincts proved correct. The business grew. Cornelia Powell had made it.

Eight or nine years after Cornelia opened her store, she found she had come to a

crossroads, and was ready to change the focus of her career. "I felt that running the business was done. I wanted to take my message to a bigger arena, maybe write a book." Personal desires also played a role in her decisions. She wanted to spend more time with her mother back in Alabama. For a time she considered closing the shop, then a friend suggested she sell it instead. At first she resisted the notion, but eventually she came to realize that what her store offered was too valuable to lose, and she did not want to disappoint her loyal patrons who were so happy with the shop's personal service and wonderful wares. "I had to look at it as a business," says Cornelia.

Though she still owns the store, Cornelia is looking for a buyer or a partner so that she does not need to be at the shop on a day-to-day basis. In the meantime, good management and invaluable staff have made it possible for her to begin the difficult process of letting go of the business and exploring some other areas of interest. She is now spreading her knowledge and expertise by giving lectures, writing for local society pages, and designing a website. These new challenges have taught her that it is always possible to build on past experience to keep your career stimulating. The decision to distance herself from the store has led to other revelations. "Letting go was part of the exercise," she says. "The business is bigger than I am."

Collecting Limoges

Debby DuBay

~

When she started collecting delicate Limoges porcelain pieces as a young woman, Debby DuBay was not thinking about her future career as an antiques dealer. She was too busy breaking ground for women serving in the United States military. She was among the first group of women recruited into the Air Force in the 1970s to meet Congressionally mandated quotas. In her 20-year military career, she received numerous decorations and commendations and achieved many firsts, including being one of the first women to go into the field of aircraft maintenance and being the first woman to give the Veteran's Day speech. But through it all, she was a reluctant pioneer for women, she says. "I just wanted to do my job, and serve my country."

Stationed in Germany when she was still a teenager, Debby began to

make side trips to Paris to visit antiques shops and combat some of the loneliness of military life. There she became entranced with Limoges porcelain—it fed her fantasies about the home she would one day have. A woman who ran one of the shops she frequented began to teach her about the art of the lovely pieces. Debby bought her first vase, and was smitten. Her purchase formed the beginnings of a collection that would become so vast she could no longer fit it into her home. Eventually, she opened a store to sell some items, and became a leading expert and dealer in Limoges.

These days, her military days behind her, Debby is ensconced in one of America's

"You have to use your uniqueness to succeed."

most scenic and historic towns, Andover, Massachusetts. It was here that she opened her small shop, Limoges Antiques, in 1995, using her extensive personal collection of Limoges porcelain as her initial inventory, to which she has added antique estate jewelry. "I wanted to do something to bring beauty to everyone who walks in the door." She knew her collection of porcelain would do just that. After all, Debby

says, "Limoges has always had an amazing ability to inspire."

Though encyclopedic in her knowledge of Limoges, Debby knew little about retail

when she first contemplated opening her shop. So she threw herself into her new

project with characteristic energy, consulting her local Small Business Administration

and other organizations for guidance, contacts, and advice on writing a business plan and

assembling all necessary legal documents. She also realized that her biggest challenge was

efficient marketing. "Because I specialize, I had to focus on my target market, collectors

and dealers of hand-painted porcelain."

Active in the Andover Historic

Society, she takes every opportunity to

promote the store, and frequently accepts

invitations to speak to other women about

"turning your passion into a profession."

Part of her message: "You have to use your

uniqueness and your personality to suc-

ceed. If you don't use it, no one else will."

Collecting the Past

MARLENE HARRIS

~

The antiques business requires not just a love of and appreciation for vintage furnishings, jewelry, and decor, but a vision of how those things can be preserved and presented in new settings. For those not steeped in antiques from childhood, it also demands a great deal of studying, reading, and learning.

Self-education was essential for Marlene Harris, a veteran antiques dealer, who taught herself about antiques through the prism of antique buttons. It was years ago, when she accompanied her husband on a business trip to New York City, that she first fell in love with beautifully crafted, painted

Hattie W. Wheeler.

W. Leon Chamberlain.

Married:

Wednesday, June 1st, 1892, Miss
Hattie W. Wheeler and Mr. W. Leon
Chamberlain, at Orange, Mass.

enamel buttons—miniature masterpieces replete with art, history, craft, and legend. "They remind us, as Charles Dickens said, that anything worth doing is worth doing well," she says. It is Marlene's exuberance and knowledge of antiques, as well as her collection of treasures, that draw customers to her tiny shop outside of Pittsburgh.

Starting her business more than two decades ago required an initial investment of $5,000, as well as the security offered by a husband who was employed. She bought as many beautiful buttons as she could, seized with the idea of transforming them into eye-catching jewelry. She donated one of her antique treasures to a charity auction, curious to see what kind of price it might fetch. At the auction, her work caught the eye of a vice president from a large local department store, and soon she was in business in earnest. For 17 years, she sold items from the Marlene Harris Collection to the department store and its branches. During this period, her husband lost his job and joined her endeavor. "My hobby had turned into the family business," she says.

Eventually, Marlene wanted more control over her hours and policies. She found herself a tiny retail space, an old chicken coop, in fact, which she transformed into a fantasy jewel box, with lace on the ceiling and fabric on the walls. Her inventory had expanded considerably, from antique and estate jewelry, to antique purses, perfume bottles, antique silver, hat pins, belt buckles, and a collection of flirtation mirrors. It helped that she had made savvy investments along the way and learned how to cope with financially lean times. During the most difficult periods Marlene survived on mail-order sales, an aspect of her business she has continued to develop with the aid of a digital camera, which enables her to e-mail pictures of items to prospective customers.

An Egg by Jane

Artist Jane Pollak designs decorative eggs and eggshell jewelry using the labor-intensive wax-and-dye method unique to Ukrainian Easter eggs. She has been selling her creations at craft shows for 15 years, and now has a direct-mail business. Her other creative and entrepreneurial endeavors include writing a book on her art, *Decorating Eggs*, and giving lectures on marketing strategies for home-based entrepreneurs and on turning a passion into a profession.

Linens

NANCY KOLTES, ALENA GERLI, & PAULA GINS

~

Just about anyone involved in the business of fine linens started out with a passion for textiles, often inherited from grandmothers or mothers who sewed, decorated their houses with delicate lace, set memorable tables, and made beds with crisp cool sheets. They are tactile people, the sort who have powerful urges to touch and work with fabric, who appreciate the handiwork involved in antique needlework, and who share a fundamental belief in exhibiting and enjoying beautiful linens rather than tucking them away in drawers.

But there are different ways to make a trade out of a love of linens: Some people yearn to design while others are satisfied to collect beautiful pieces from around the world for resale. Nancy Koltes, a New York–based designer of luxurious bed linens, is a canny businesswoman who has grown a company from the ground up, and now employs 35 people. Alena Ovesna Gerli brings her European heritage and expertise to the collection, design, and manufacture of high-quality linens for bed and table in her Pleasantville, New York, company, White Linen. Paula Gins in Littleton, Colorado, has turned her discerning eye for fine European antique linens into a one-woman venture that keeps her busy with buying trips, washing, ironing, and one-on-one consultations with clients.

A business idea is often borne out of adversity and necessity. Nancy Koltes started her own business when the job that had brought her to New York fell through. "I had to do something," she said. "So, I started designing." After a few years, when she began to notice that some of the patterns she

designed were requested over and over again, she developed a wholesale collection. Orders

began to pour in, and to fill them she needed to expand. Her company has kept grow-

ing, and now manufactures several lines of linens, from a casual, youthful line to classic

comforters, cashmere throw blankets, and luxurious towels. She even has a line of bath

products. "I've always been interested in doing more," she says, admitting that her focus

has shifted with the growth of her business from the creative to the administrative.

The hardest part, she says, has always been financing. Initially, she got capital from

family and friends. "It's very difficult for a woman to get capital from a bank, particu-

"Starting a business is very far from anything romantic."

larly in the soft goods business like things for the home," she says. But she preferred

autonomy and even poverty to being indebted or beholden to investors. "You need

tremendous perseverance, sacrifice, and dedication. You have to do whatever it takes."

To some extent, it was Alena Ovesna Gerli's alienation from the world of fashion

and the politics of New York's Seventh Avenue that propelled her into starting her own

company. "I grew up in a Communist country, Czechoslovakia," she says. "I don't know

where I got my free spirit. I have always had a yearning to be free, whether it's from

Communism or from an obnoxious boss."

Fortunately, Alena's yearning came in the early eighties, a time when the home furnishings market was taking off. She started her company by investing her own savings in high-end Italian sheets. "My idea was that we would have a small collection and have everything in stock so that we could deliver within a few days," she says.

"To this day, this is one of our basic premises: fast delivery." It is one that she says separates her company from its competitors.

The beginning was tough, though. It took time to establish White Linen in

the trade, to grow the collection and generate enough cash flow to pay for expanding the inventory with, for instance, antique reproductions. "Starting a business is very far from anything romantic,"

Alena says. "We went for six or seven years without taking a vacation. My husband credits my success with stubborn perseverance."

Paula Gins began her own business when she and her husband moved to Colorado. The nature of her company, buying and reselling European antique linens circa

"It has worked out to be very fulfilling."

1820-1900, keeps it small, and to her mind extremely rewarding. With a constantly revolving inventory culled from several buying trips a year, she sells by appointment out of her home, takes part in several annual antiques shows, and regularly sees her fabulous collection featured in magazines. Initially investing about

$8,000 of her own money, she poured her profits back into the business. Though she admits that she doesn't get paid for the time she spends washing and ironing her perfect pieces, she is obviously content. "It has worked out to be very fulfilling," she says.

The biggest challenge—and the biggest satisfaction—for Paula has been educating her clients about what they are buying, since each piece she carries is rich with detail and history. "I want people to know what they are looking at," she says. "My hang tags have a complete description." Above all, she encourages customers to touch the linens, to share her intimacy with the pieces she cherishes.

The Pillowmaker

With a business card, an 800 phone number, and a website, Kathe Williams began her own full-fledged business, The Pillowmaker. She makes pillows out of fabric scraps  that her customers cannot part with—monogrammed sheets, tapestries, wedding gowns, college sweatshirts. Clients are encouraged to design the pillows themselves, but if they lack inspiration Kathe will gladly take the initiative and custom-design the pillows herself.

Shedding Light

JOYCE AMES LAMPSHADES

~

Joyce Ames is a designer who has built a six-figure business out of designing and making lampshades covered with a rich variety of antique cloth, trims, and tassels; designs that are inspired by history. Part of Joyce's success stems from the fact that she has been able to educate her customers on the importance of light, and lamplight in particular, in room design.

Her 32-year-old business is a grand marriage of two of her passions, antique fabrics and lampshades. Mechanical by nature—"I dream in three dimensions," she says—Joyce learned how to put together a lampshade by taking old ones apart. Fabric is to her what paint is to

other artists; it's her medium, and she knows it intimately. She'll cover a lampshade

in fabric from floral curtains, old bedspreads, chintz, or lace, all as sturdy as they

are romantic. Sewing from the time she was five, she honed her skills and

knowledge buying and selling lace in Europe in her twenties.

But she didn't start out making lampshades for people to buy. She made her living

designing sets for period movies and magazine photo shoots, wherever fabric was

needed as part of an interior design. "I was the one who got the job done," she says,

explaining her success. Her work for magazines helped expand her reputation, so that

when she started her own line of shades in between movie jobs, her name was already

well known. Magazines featured articles about her, word of her talent spread, and before

too long she landed a huge contract making lampshades for Ralph Lauren. "Everyone

in lampshades knows me," she says, brimming with the confidence that comes with a

certain maturity as a businesswoman.

When her business took off in 1989, Joyce was tempted to expand, but opted

not to, in order to maintain tight control and stay lean and mean. "Thank goodness

I did not expand," she says now, "because the Gulf War hit and the recession came

and I would have been out of business." One of the lessons she derives from this experience: "It's not necessary to expand just because you have a little business. You have to have a rent you can live with in the slow times."

There are other benefits to keeping her business relatively small in size, Joyce says, even when financial security made expansion a possibility. It preserves her creative control, and enables her to maintain the dreaming time so vital to any artist. She has staff in her studio only on Tuesdays through Thursdays, leaving her Mondays and Fridays free to putter and come up with new designs, finish projects, and tie up any loose ends.

Like a true artist, Joyce's work stems from a "desperation not to be mediocre." She is certain her success lies in her dedication to beauty and superior quality. "I'm the ultimate gambler," she says. "I don't test-market. If I know it's beautiful, I make it and it sells." How does she know? "Because I never make anything that I wouldn't personally have in my home. If you make something beautiful, they will come."

$\mathcal{G}$rowing With Grace

$\mathcal{E}$xpanding and growing are considered the natural and desired course of business, but not everyone who goes into business wants to preside over a vast empire. For an entrepreneur who is also a designer, such as Joyce Ames, growing takes time and energy that was once spent creating, and this means taking over other, more administrative, tasks. For some, the prospect of expanding is a delicious challenge with a tantalizing potential payoff for years of hard work. Others find, sometimes in retrospect, that although their business has grown, the passion that once fueled it has become diluted in the process.

Like anything with a potential upside, expanding your business is a risk, and many successful entrepreneurs recommend holding back, growing slowly, and being conservative. Just because one large order has come in does not guarantee that they will keep coming in. Just because a store is successful in one location does not mean that a similar one will be successful in another location. Hiring new staff and increasing your overhead are decisions that you have to live with well beyond filling the next order. It's important to know when and how to expand, and these decisions should be as well researched as the decision to open a business in the first place.

No one can run a huge or even medium-sized company by herself, so expansion also entails having the right team in place. This means people you trust to run and perform aspects of your business for which you have neither the time nor inclination. Growing larger inevitably means delegating more tasks, and some loss of creative control. For some people, the process of letting go of certain aspects of a business they have nurtured since infancy can be as painful as it is necessary.

PART TWO

Dollars & Sense

$\mathcal{Y}$our dreams and your grit have taken you far, but as your business matures, you realize that running an enterprise takes even more than that. You have learned the basics—keeping records, setting realistic goals, finding a source of financing, and hiring staff. No longer a neophyte, you have the benefit of experience. The hardest part—the leap into the unknown—is behind you, and there is no substitute for what you have learned running your business hands-on.

Now it is time to refine your skills, maybe by taking some business courses to help plan your next venture. Perhaps you want to take your business in a different direction. Perhaps you want to explore your options for expanding and for improving your revenues. A few years into any business is a time to take stock, to strategize for the future, to re-examine givens, to make sure that, bottom line, the business makes dollars and sense.

THE ESSENTIALS

Owning a business means making a steady stream of decisions large and small. Will you distribute your product wholesale or retail or by mail order? How big do you want to grow? Is it important for you have to have total control over every aspect of your enterprise? Can you delegate some tasks? Are you in it for artistic fulfillment? Or do you want to make it big in terms of profits?

The decision-making process is never laid to rest. As your company grows, it calls for constant refinement and realistic assessment. Where are the weaknesses? Are you reaching clients as well as you should? Presenting your product in the best possible light?

Not every business is destined to be huge, and it is even conceivable that one day you will grow out of your labor of love and decide to move on. You may reach the point where you'll consider selling your company or taking it in a new direction.

The following are profiles of businesswomen at different stages who faced the hard decisions.

$\mathcal{G}$rowing

KAREN SKELTON

~

No one could have been more surprised than Karen Skelton when her pottery business, something she had started almost as a lark, began to take off.

Karen had been working as a graphic designer in New York City, doing mostly product design, when she decided to take a pottery class. The concrete, hand-dirtying business of making pots and experimenting with glazing was the perfect counterpoint to her more corporate day job, which she describes as the "world of presentations." She enjoyed applying her fine sense of color to something so immediate and organic, almost primitive. When a friend invited her to display her wares at the New York Gift Show, where stores come to order goods, she figured she had nothing to lose. At the show she took in orders for 7,000 pots. "Then I pretty much had to do it," she recalls. "I had

to build a studio. I had to learn everything."

Faced with a huge order, Karen had to rely on the patience of her clients, who needed to be called when orders ran late. A natural experimenter, Karen could not always reproduce precise hues, so pieces tended to be one-of-a-kind and unpre-

"People fall in love with what I do. That feels great."

dictable. But the flower stores and other gift and craft shops were seldom disappointed. They loved her flower pots in glazes the color of earth and sky—a palette that included amber, wheat, butter, and periwinkle—all perfectly complementing whatever flowers they might hold, and as sturdy as they were beautiful.

To keep building her business, Karen used the knowledge she had accumulated from previous work experience. She had learned a good deal about marketing from her jobs in advertising. She is a skilled photographer, so she made beautiful color postcards of her pots and other creations to use as her catalogue and calling card.

She knew how to design a logo, and gave her new venture the catchy double entendre Potluck Studios. Her work ethic, which she attributes to her midwestern upbringing and an entrepreneurial father who taught her that even when you don't know what to do, you should still do something, also  came into play. "All of this helped," Karen says. "But the best thing was having this wonderful thing to make and sell."

She found the perfect place to do just that, opening a studio and store in the sleepy little picturesque village of Accord, in New York's Catskill mountains (and just a two-hour drive for her all-important annual Gift Show selling sojourn). The beautiful surroundings are a perfect backdrop to her store, where pottery is displayed in antique, weathered cupboards and on tables, which are also for sale. Shoppers tend to cart off armloads of Karen's colorful clay creations, along with the pillows, linens, and soaps she has begun to sell.

With nine employees now, Karen has expanded into making country-style tableware, clay creations adorned with her unique glowing, brilliant-colored finishes. "Colors are what people love," she says. "People fall in love with what I do. That feels great."

Summer Cottage

Beth Moorin began Summer Cottage when, unable to find affordable cabinet pulls for her new house, she decided to create her own. The results were so beautiful that she began to sell her  botanically inspired knobs at craft shows in Atlanta. Now Beth sells to over 150 retail shops around the country, and has expanded her collection to include candlesticks, switchplates, picture frames, stools, and floorcloths in over 45 different patterns.

Your Business Plan

It takes more than a vision to hang out a shingle. What it takes is a business plan, a written blueprint that will not only provide you with a guide for making decisions, but will offer important information to all those interested in your company—bankers, lawyers, potential partners, investors, accountants—who will need to know the specifics of your company, financial and otherwise.

Your business plan should define your idea, product, or service, who the potential buyer or user will be, and who your competition is. You must have clearly thought out how you will market and sell your concept: Will you sell retail, mail order, or wholesale? What is your advertising and publicity strategy? What is the image your company will convey? What experiences and skills make you the perfect person to start this new company? Where will you get the start-up capital for your enterprise?

Most experts advise entrepreneurs to plan ten years into the future, and your plan should specify your goals for each year: When do you expect to break even? When do you need a positive cash flow? Remember to provide as many specific examples as possible on all aspects, including financial, of your company. If starting a business seems a dreamy prospect, the plan is an exercise in realism and conservatism, the impetus to pay close attention to all the details.

A good source for guidance is the *Business Plan Handbook*, a compilation of actual plans developed by small businesses throughout North America. Local Small Business Development Centers are also extremely helpful and provide templates for business plans. Also, don't be shy about seeking mountains of advice from other entrepreneurs you admire.

Floral Visions

~

Though her dried flower creations are as whimsical as they are lovely, Beth Siqueland-Gresch approached the opening of her own shop anything but lightly. The shop, called Grasmere, in Barrington, Rhode Island, was the fruit of no less than six years of careful planning and research on the part of this former art and art history student. After working in visual display for a large retailing corporation, Beth knew the corporate life was not for her and that she wanted to open her own business. To learn the ropes, she apprenticed herself to a series of floral and horticulture businesses, studied up on the mechanics of

running a small business, and scrimped and saved some start-up money.

When she was almost ready to open her shop, she took her arrangements to a few craft shows to see what the response would be, and it was overwhelmingly favorable. Then she opened her doors in a renovated 1930s gray clapboard

"*It's about finding a way to do what you love.*"

farmhouse as a retailer of some ready-made creations but, even more, as a custom designer. Beth offers rather unusual solutions to interior-design dilemmas. Customers love her topiary dividers, and her custom-sized wreaths—made of such elements as parchment fruits and roses—which add three-dimensional drama to a spot where a painting might otherwise hang.

Beth's first year was tough, both more work-intensive and more cash-intensive than she had anticipated. But by the second year, as she gained experience and confidence, Beth managed to turn a small profit, and succeeding years have brought more returns. She has diversified somewhat, and has taken on more special events and weddings than before, but the core of the business is still the custom-designed dried flower creations that she and her loyal customers love. Still, she acknowledges, "This kind of business will never make me wealthy. It's more about finding a way to do what you love, and making a sustainable income doing it."

Hannah's Treasures

Marilyn Krehbiel learned how to make bandboxes while working at her sister's company, Box Lore. She jumped at the chance to take over this specialized business when her sister wanted to try something new. The result was Marilyn's very own company, Hannah's Treasures, which manufactures hatboxes, trays, children's hangers, and, of course, bandboxes, which are covered with vintage wallpaper and lined inside with antique newsprint circa 1890-1948.

Selling by Post

WHISPERING PINES

~

Childhood memories exert a powerful pull, all the more so when you multiply by two. Sisters Mickey Kelly and Susan Kelly Panian were living in separate parts of the country when they decided to join in a business venture that would reconnect them—and a lot of other people—with a cherished aspect of their past. When they were growing up in Chicago, they would escape in the summers to their family cabin in the sleepy little hamlet of Three Lakes, Wisconsin (population 300). It had left an indelible mark on both women's imaginations, filling them with warm remembrances of summers spent perfectly in tune with nature and themselves.

Mickey, the elder sister by three years, first had the vision. She opened a store in her adopted hometown of Piermont, New York, called

Whispering Pines, which was reminiscent of the trading posts the girls had frequented in Three Lakes. Specializing in "things for the cabin," Whispering Pines carried everything from Adirondack twig furniture and beaded moccasins to outdoor clothing and souvenir pillows filled with fragrant pine needles. The idea was to create that "cabin state of mind" even for those without cabins. Susan followed Mickey's lead and opened a similar store in Delray Beach, Florida. Together the sisters opened a third store in Three Lakes, where they still summer with their families.

The stores were a success, but it wasn't long before Mickey and Susan found themselves with a bad case of retail burnout. They put their heads together to figure out how to escape the day-to-day demands of running a store yet still be able to connect with a wide circle of customers. The solution: transform Whispering Pines into a mail-order catalogue business. They already had thousands of names of customers who had expressed eagerness for a catalogue if they ever produced one; they obtained additional names from a list broker. The catalogue was designed by Susan's husband, Ed, a graphic designer, who selected cream-colored, linen-textured, recycled paper, which was expensive but had just the right feel. In 1993, fueled more by instinct than any concrete plan, they mailed their first catalogue, uncertain of the outcome.

Calls flooded in, and relatives and friends were recruited to take orders and pack the merchandise off. "We were like Lucy and Ethel in the chocolate factory," says Susan. "We were surrounded by boxes." Friends with children worked part-time at the family-friendly company. As the business grew, the sisters strove to keep it quirky, personal, and home-spun. The following year they won a prestigious award from the Direct Marketing Association for their catalogue, no mean feat in a crowded mail-order field. As they

went along, they refined the business, learning for instance that some products are more successful in stores than in catalogues. "By the time we put out the second catalogue, we figured we were committed," says Mickey, still sounding a

bit surprised by their success. The transition from store to catalogue had worked, and though they still push themselves incredibly hard—hauling boxes themselves when necessary—they find the work more gratifying than ever. One advantage: "Even as your

circulation grows," says Susan, "your product, the catalogue, essentially remains the same."

Although the business has expanded and relocated to Fairfield, Connecticut, it remains very much a family affair. Susan's husband continues as art director, the kids model for the catalogue, and various relatives lend a helping hand during the

company's most frantic season, around the Christmas holidays. Spring is also a busy time, as people prepare to stock up summer houses. The sisters have complementary talents and roles in the company. "Mickey," Susan says, "is our visionary. She does a lot of the buying." Susan, on the other hand, is the operations person, carefully scrutinizing numbers, solving problems, and collaborating with Mickey to set the tone and direction of the catalogue. Above all, they both agree, "We've had a lot of fun."

Mail-Order Tips

*E*veryone loves getting packages in the mail, and people have less and less time to shop. These two truths have led to an explosion in the mail-order and catalogue business in recent years. There are obvious advantages to selling your wares this way. For one thing, you're not tethered to the responsibilites of running a store. For another, you can sell higher-price merchandise, as consumers are generally willing to pay more for the convenience of mail-order. But be prepared to join a crowd. The *Directory of Mail-Order Catalogs* lists about 500 new businesses per year, most of them tiny. About 300 of these businesses are deleted the following year. Here are some tips to help you beat the odds:

~ **Maintain your mailing list.** Clean it out periodically. People move a lot. Keep a record of your regular customers, and if your product is highly personal, you might want to keep additional information on your customers, like significant life-cycle events, marriages, births.

~ **Make it easy to get on your list.** Include a registration form in each mailing.

~ **Ask customers where they heard about you.** This information tells you the most effective way of reaching potential customers.

~ **Interview a list broker,** who can recommend lists culled from other catalogue companies with markets similar to yours.

~ **Start small,** perhaps with a little brochure instead of a catalogue.

~ **Investigate printing houses** since prices, service, and quality can vary wildly. For a catalogue, you need the best of all three.

~ **Design your catalogue to stand out from the pack.** Archivia, the Madison Avenue decorative arts bookshop, has an odd-sized square catalogue with black and white photos. Whispering Pines, the Connecticut-based outfit that sells "things for the cabin," has won awards for its catalogue, which is printed on a linen-color paper.

~ **Consider charging for your catalogue.** This helps identify serious buyers. When someone places an order, you can subtract the price of the catalogue from the total order.

~ **Be responsible about filling orders.** The shorter your response time, the better.

~ **Hire well-informed operators** who are efficient but can also answer customers' questions.

~ **Respond to and take note of complaints.** Don't keep shipping out an item that repeatedly disappoints people.

~ **Consider your packaging.** It should be witty and thoughtful but sturdy enough to not get damaged in the mail.

~ **Follow up** with a letter or card to determine the customer's satisfaction and garner suggestions for other items.

~ **A mail-order business should be accessible** by phone, fax, or e-mail.

~ **Offer changing selections,** new items, and customized services. This is what will set you apart from the competition.

Keeping Shop

MARSTON HOUSE &
TANCREDI & MORGEN

~

Back in the mid-eighties, it would have been difficult for Marsha Alldis to envision the life she has today. She felt as though she was hitting bottom. Though she had run a fabric shop in Carmel, California, and had worked in fashion design, she had nothing in the way of financial resources to show for it all, and was feeling unfulfilled.

But within a relatively short span of time, every facet of her life would change. She met and married Roger Alldis, an engineer from South Africa, became pregnant with twin girls at the age of 40, and—when she discovered that a nearby shop she admired was for sale—decided she would like to be the store's owner. She and her husband purchased Tancredi & Morgen, a charming store in a red barn outside of town, from Sharon and Paul

Mrozinski, a couple who were relocating to Maine to start another business. The negotiation was friendly: Marsha had no money from her other business, so it was established that payments would be made over time out of the profits she earned at the store. If payments ran late, Sharon would simply take back some

inventory Even so, there were some difficult periods. About the time they opened their doors, Marsha gave birth to her girls, Megan and Gwyneth. "Everything blossomed at once," says Marsha. "There were days when that was hard to handle."

"Everything blossomed at once . . . That was hard to handle."

In the beginning, Marsha and her husband, who gave up his engineering career to join her in the enterprise, took it one day at a time. Working with whatever cash flow they could muster, Marsha slowly transformed the shop to suit her personal and eclectic taste. It has grown every year of the twelve years they have owned it. Today, it features a mixture of American and European country-style antiques, Marsha's line of sophisticated bohemian clothing, and a full array of soothing herbs. "In reality, there's nothing in our store that anyone absolutely needs to survive," she says. "It's the way we put it together, the comforting atmosphere. We keep the business very personal."

Marsha and Roger also throw two or three parties a year under a tent in the backyard, inviting their entire mailing list and drawing 500 to 600 people. The parties—which might have themes like "Paris" or "Phantom of the Opera"—also feature artists' booths and have proved to be great for sales and for getting the word out about the store. The twins, who have grown up in the store and are now twelve, help decorate. "We'll do more business that day than we will for a month."

Although her background is artistic, Marsha says she loves the challenge and motivation of setting business goals for herself, and she credits Roger with encouraging her to take a longer view of the business. "We share a philosophy," she says, which includes staying current with their bills and being flexible in

times of difficulty. "Now, after we've become established, we have inner strength that we can count on."

Sharon Mrozinski describes the sensation of picking up her California stakes to move to a long-neglected but historic property on the coast of Maine as one fueled by a childhood dream. Despite being raised in the West and living for years in California, she had always felt her sensibilities meshed with life in New England, and had planned to retire there someday. She loved the antiquities, the sense of place, the history, and the frugality. When she and her husband, Paul, an architect, found a piece of property they could not resist, a 1785 Federal house on Main Street in Wiscasset, Maine, they decided to pursue her fantasy. Sharon's departure from California was helped by the fact that the business she had built there was passing into the trusted hands of Marsha Alldis. Either way, though, Sharon and her husband were committed.

Sharon and Paul had their work cut out for them. With about $25,000 in savings,

they set about bringing the Marston House back to life. They planned a garden-oriented antiques shop in the main house, and converted the carriage house in back into a bed and breakfast. "We thought we'd do whatever it took to make it," says Sharon. "We had a lot of innocence. That helps immensely."

"We had a lot of innocence. That helps immensely."

They opened the shop on July 4, 1987, and the event was a big success. The Mrozinskis had savvily bought the Maine Antique Dealers New England mailing list and sent off 10,000 announcements, so a large number of antiques dealers and collectors flocked to the picturesque house.

What Sharon and Paul had not quite

counted on were the extremes of the climate in their new home, where the selling and tourist seasons are shorter than they had expected. "We discovered we were in Maine in the middle of winter with our knickers down," says Sharon. "We had some very scary moments."

To cope, Sharon and Paul implemented a variety of strategies: packing up and doing some antiques shows off-season, learning the seasonal rhythm of farming and working hard all summer to save up for the winter, and getting a credit line from a local bank. The Marston House became a showcase for Paul, who took on some architectural projects to tide them over.

Despite the challenges, Sharon has no regrets. "The ability to let go and follow your heart is the purest form of faith," she says. "You need to free-fall and find your place."

$\mathcal{L}$ocation, Location

$\mathcal{L}$ocation can make all the difference in just about any kind of business. For a store, the importance is obvious. It needs to be accessible and visible to shoppers. An address on Madison Avenue in New York or Melrose Avenue in Hollywood benefits from upscale street traffic and surroundings, but of course, you'll pay a premium for such fashionable quarters. A shop in a picturesque town, such as Limoges in Andover, Massachusetts, or Carol Bolton's six-store empire in tiny Fredericksburg, Texas, may be off the beaten track, but the towns attract antique-loving tourists looking to part with their money.

Even when the enterprise is not a store, its whereabouts can matter. Its location can set the tone and make it an appealing place to work, hence attracting the best possible staff. For wholesalers, reasonable proximity to trade or craft shows, suppliers, and other vital aspects of their industry are a consideration. Karen Skelton's Potluck Studios might have the best of both worlds. It's situated in a quaint little mountain village, but is close enough to New York City for the annual sales trip to the New York Gift Show.

Another growing trend for small businesses is to set up offices, studios, and shops in a business incubator. These centers are designed specifically for start-up businesses and are located throughout North America. They provide low-rent space, shared office equipment such as fax and photocopying machines, business services, and counseling on how to develop and expand small companies. Though most business incubators are nonprofit organizations, their success has led to the birth of many privately owned versions.

Shop Interiors

The feel of shop interiors varies depending on what is being sold, of course, but customers like to understand immediately what the style, quality, and price range of the store is. Creative design elements—lighting, music, flowers, packaging, scents, window and in-store displays—all help to convey a general image. Find inspiration in other stores that cater to the same market, and flip through design magazines for ideas. Here are some tips for making a shop comfortable and welcoming.

- Let no space be left unconsidered. Walls, floors, ceiling, even doorknobs should all be part of the store's overall style.
- Display items for inspiration—a scarf filling a neckline of a dress; an urn filled with a dozen hydrangeas.
- Place pretty impulse items by the register.
- Create a place where customers can sit, relax, and linger for a while.
- Consider an amenity like a pitcher of fresh juice or a hot cup of tea for shoppers.
- Keep the layout of the store manageable so that cleaning is never a huge obstacle.
- Make clothing racks accessible—not too low, high, or crowded.

POOLING
TALENTS

No one is great at absolutely everything. And no one succeeds in business completely

alone. When family members join in an endeavor, there is unexpected satisfaction in

knowing that your business has provided for the people closest to you—provided them

with a means to shine and a means of income. Along the way, there are new discover-

ies of the hidden talents of loved ones.

Many small businesses have the feel of family, whether the participants are

actually related or not. Working well together, sometimes in close quarters for long

stretches of time, builds a sort of bond that is difficult to match, and is integral to the

workings of any small enterprise.

Perhaps your spouse will be the ideal business partner. Perhaps a sister, or even

your mother, will have the needed skills that you yourself lack. Or perhaps your

family business is harder to quantify: It might be the quality time together that

makes the most sense.

Partners for Life

TRACY & JOHN PORTER

~

It generally is not considered advisable to embark on three of life's great adventures—and three of life's most stressful undertakings—all at the same time. But that is more or less what Tracy and John Porter, both former fashion models with energy to spare, did back in 1991 when they moved, married, and started a business together in the space of about one month's time. The Porters left downtown Chicago for what Tracy calls "a darling little farm" that sits on 26 acres outside Princeton, Wisconsin. There, they started Stonehouse Farm Goods in a converted chicken coop. The homey little company has since developed into a multifaceted housewares and furniture design empire.

Tracy had always been creative, making purses, jewelry, and pottery in the basement of her Chicago row house and selling her creations piecemeal through small local stores. When a handpainted tray she gave to a friend at a bridal shower elicited intense "oohs" and "ahs" and requests for more, something clicked. Without a formal business plan yet in place, she and John, about to marry, decided to try to wholesale her whimsically painted wares. Borrowing $5,000 from Tracy's parents, they headed off to the Gift Show in New York City. They figured they would consider the trade show a success if they sold at least $10,000 worth of goods. They came home with $74,000 worth of orders to fill.

With neither a studio nor staff, the prospect they faced was at first overwhelming. Luckily, both possess a can-do temperament, and they ploughed through the work. "John was base-coating and polyurethaning and I was painting," says Tracy. Those were heady days. Before long they had converted their new farm to a manufacturing operation—they erected a new studio and hired 50 employees, including local artisans.

John settled into a role on the business side, handling financial matters such as accounting and cash flow. Tracy, forever the designer, has not come close to running out of ideas for their many products, from rugs and dinnerware to greeting cards. She even began to design the company's wholesale catalogue, and oversees marketing and public relations and develops what she calls the company's "big picture." Both husband and wife agree that their company is their baby. "In the beginning we both wanted to do every-

"It's important that we both can take constructive criticism."

thing and we had to divide up the tasks," Tracy says. "It's hard to have all the input you want when you grow so fast." Seven years into both the marriage and the business, they

have traveled lots of road together. "Working with your spouse is not always an easy thing to do," she adds. "You think you know someone until you see how they are when they conduct business. It's important that we can both take constructive criticism."

Not long ago, Tracy and John came to

a crossroads in their business and decided to move away from manufacturing and into licensing their designs. "It was a difficult decision to make—we had to let a lot of people go—but it was the right decision for us," says Tracy. "Manufacturing is not our true love. Designing and creating a look is." Now, down to an aggressive, efficient team of ten, they make furniture only for their own store, Stonehouse Farm Goods: The Store, a showcase for Tracy's designs in Princeton, Wisconsin. Much of Tracy's energy now goes into their newest venture, Tracy Porter: The Home Collection, which includes hooked rugs, pillows, and throws. They have numerous licensing deals with manufacturers as Tracy's name grows into a fixture in the housewares design field.

Tracy and John have made a point of learning as much as they can about each aspect of their combined venture. For every move they've made, they've consulted experts in the field. But even with all the advice, says Tracy, "You still have to make the decision. You have to go with your gut."

An Expert Team

When you start a business, you need a trusted lawyer, accountant, and financial advisor as part of your expert business team. Business laws are extremely complicated, and a lawyer can guide you through miles of red tape. Professional legal advice may be expensive, but all entrepreneurs agree it is absolutely essential and can save you money in the long run. A lawyer can also advise you on what kinds of insurance you need and where you might be vulnerable to a lawsuit. An accountant and financial planner can deal with complicated tax issues and regulations and help you plan for long-range financial goals, such as retirement.

As you conduct your business, there will be numerous legal contracts and financial transactions for which you will require expert advice. Don't just hire any lawyer or accountant. Look for a team that specializes in your type of small business—whether it's wholesale, licensing, or retail—and with whom you feel comfortable. You will, after all, be dealing with them quite often. Ask lots of questions—remember, knowledge is power. Each contract and transaction will be a learning experience, the lessons to be incorporated into the next one. If you would like your understanding of business to go beyond the basics, consider taking college courses in small business law or accounting, or attend classes and workshops at a local chapter of the Small Business Development Center.

Once you have assembled a trustworthy group of advisors, consult them whenever needed. But the fact is that no one knows your business as well as you, or spends more time thinking about it. Don't hand over the really big decisions—legal, financial, or otherwise—to anyone else.

Mother & Daughter

AMBIE HAY JR. AND SR.

~

The eldest daughter in a Kentucky family of nine children, Ambie Hay Jr. has always been particularly close to her mother, Ambie Hay Sr. Not only do they share a first name that has come down through several generations of the family's maternal line, they share an artistic predilection and an abiding interest in antiques and crafts.

And, for the past few years, this mother and daughter have had even more to discuss. The two women each own and run similar but separate shops stocked with charming items for the home: painted furniture,

fabric, fringed floral pillows, prints, linens, scented candles, and more.

Sometimes daughters follow in their mother's footsteps, but it was Ambie Jr. who pioneered their business. She fell in love with the idyllic island of Nantucket after a summer baby-sitting job brought her there, and opened a tiny shop right on the water-

front to sell her painted furniture. She named the store Rosa Rugosa, after the rugged beach rose that is native to Nantucket. After pitching in for a while in her daughter's store, which was rapidly expanding into housewares and furniture, and finding that she rather enjoyed that kind of work, Ambie Sr. was inspired to open

"I really like the fact that we each have our own stores."

her own store, Ambrosia's Garden, in Delray Beach, Florida, where she had moved.

Being in two different places for part of the year has not curtailed the women's intimacy. "We talk about five times a day," says Ambie Jr. "I really like the fact that we each have our own stores. It gives us a connection but also some distance." Ambie Sr. agrees

that they have found the perfect balance: "It's special that she has her thing and I have mine."

The two women still spend plenty of time together in person. When things get slow in the summer months in Florida, Ambie Sr. comes north to Nantucket to pitch in at her daughter's shop, now housed in a 2,000-square-foot historic barn on Main Street. When the Nantucket selling season slows to a halt, Ambie Jr. packs up and moves to Vero Beach, Florida, where she has opened a second store. The two women antique together, attend gift shows, and exchange endless busi-

ness notes. Ambie Jr. and her mother refer customers to one another and share sources, suppliers, a love of meeting local artists and craftspeople, and the view that their work is their ultimate passion.

Other family members help out as well, says Ambie Jr., who has borrowed money for the business from family when needed, being careful to

repay them promptly. Brothers who are handy (one lives in Nantucket and one lives in Florida) help the women hang signs, drive trucks, lend tools, and do carpentry. Ambie Jr. says she always makes sure to pay them for their time since it is, after all, business.

One tiny regret, says Ambie Jr., is that with the growth of her business, she seldom has time for her first love, painting. Still, she recognizes that she does not quite have the temperament of a full-time artist. "I love painting, but I don't always like being alone in my studio," she explains. During her short, fast, hectic season, it is all she and her staff can do to keep up with the demand.

There have even been offers to expand the business far beyond the women's wildest imaginings. "We had some people who wanted to invest and put stores like ours around the country," said Ambie Sr. "We decided not to do that. So many things are one of a kind. If there were stores all over the country, they would lose authenticity."

Still, Ambie Sr. wouldn't mind if there was one more store in the family. She's been trying to convince another daughter to open one—so far, to no avail.

$\mathcal{G}$etting the Word Out

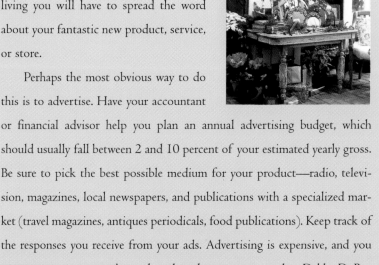

$\mathcal{L}$aboring in obscurity is not the formula for success in any business, large or small. One way or another, in order to make a living you will have to spread the word about your fantastic new product, service, or store.

Perhaps the most obvious way to do this is to advertise. Have your accountant or financial advisor help you plan an annual advertising budget, which should usually fall between 2 and 10 percent of your estimated yearly gross. Be sure to pick the best possible medium for your product—radio, television, magazines, local newspapers, and publications with a specialized market (travel magazines, antiques periodicals, food publications). Keep track of the responses you receive from your ads. Advertising is expensive, and you want to get your money's worth and reach your target market. Debby DuBay took this tack with her Limoges antiques shop: "The first year I advertised in everything. The second year, I advertised only in those publications that I got responses from."

Every businessperson needs to be media savvy. Hiring a publicist who knows which magazines and media outlets cover your particular business is not a bad idea, at least at the outset. But you yourself will probably be the best promoter of your business. Your unique touches may be the most effective form of advertising. New York interior designer Charlotte Moss made the bold move of inviting appropriate magazine editors, one at a time, to tea when she first opened a store. She has since been featured in many interior design magazines, which has given her incredible amounts of exposure.

Another fun way to get the word out about a new store or business is to throw a Grand Opening party. Invite as many people as you can handle—friends, relatives, local business owners, neighbors. If you have the space for a really large function, consider putting an ad in the local papers with an open invitation to the community. Parties are a great opportunity to spread goodwill about your business, and they need not be expensive. Barter with neighboring businesses, offering them free publicity in exchange for refreshments, entertainment, or flowers.

Some businesses find these events so successful they host parties on a regular basis. Conni Cross holds an annual Christmas Fair, selling holiday wreaths, plants, and antiques. This allows her to celebrate the season with clients and make sales during what would otherwise be a slow winter season in the garden-design business. Rebecca Black, owner of the beautiful 17-acre Foxglove Farm, which sells dried flower arrangements in British Columbia, holds an annual two-day Fall Fair, sending invitations to customers on her mailing list and encouraging them to bring friends. Featuring music, workshops, and antiques, the event draws a few thousand people, is great publicity, and enables Rebecca to sell a lot of her creations.

A Family Affair

THE GREY HAVENS INN

~

It has the makings of a Disney movie. Two generations of a colorful Texas family, each with five kids spaced about two years apart, transplanted and raised according to the seasonal rhythms of life at a classic turn-of-the-century Maine inn. At The Grey Havens Inn on Georgetown Island, near the shipbuilding capital of Bath, the view is breathtaking and wild, the salt air tangy, and the sleeping and eating better than anywhere else in the world.

At least it seems so to Hilda Hardcastle, who years ago, as a Dallas housewife and mother with a larger-than-life personality, fell in love with Maine and decided she had to have piece of it. She modestly figured running an inn fell within her abilities. "It's a matter of cleaning toilets, making beds, and keeping people under one roof from killing each other,"

she says. She searched for just the right property for years, and finally bought The Grey Havens in 1976. While the building was relatively intact, it needed a major decorating overhaul. Hilda set to work and restored the lounge with its huge stone fireplace, made curtains, and scoured nearby villages for quilts, rockers, and iron beds

"Families running businesses have to get along."

to fill the thirteen guest rooms. The children, mostly teenagers by then, pitched in with painting, carpentry, laundry, cleaning, and breakfast-making, activities that kept

them occupied from dawn to dusk. "That inn raised my kids," says Hilda, who in her time was known to float down the staircase in her nightgown to play the piano

and sing with guests. "To this day, they are the most amazingly close kids."

But the children grew up as children do, and moved on with their lives. Hilda found that running the inn without them was hard and lonely work. Then something totally unexpected happened. Her middle child, Haley, brought her then-fiance Bill Eberhart to the inn for a visit. He immediately fell in love with it and convinced Haley that they were destined to run it. "Growing up, we called it The Grey Havens curse," jokes Haley. "A month after you think you've left it behind, that place starts to haunt you." Haley and Bill finally bought it from Hilda in 1991, in the midst of creating their own family of five children. The children, like their mother before them, help out with chores and charm the guests.

Running the inn is a seasonal business, as most are in Maine. The Eberharts have extended the season from April to October, to get as much as income as possible out of the inn. Bill is a partner with a brother-in-law in another business as well, a lobster

pound and outdoor restaurant nearby. The family stays in the inn through Christmas, then closes it down for three months and "reads good books," says Haley, in Florida. Haley decided to homeschool all of the children, a decision she researched thoroughly and which Haley proudly admits is working beautifully. One child is a gifted writer, she says. Another has a talent for golf. On a practical level, thanks to their Maine summers, all of them know how to pump water from a well.

Getting through the winter is tough—much depends on having a good August. March and April are always the lean months, when every dollar is stretched. "I have a wonderful husband," says Haley. "That's a crucial ingredient. Families running businesses have to get along."

Hilda Hardcastle has never gotten over her love affair with Maine. She settled in nearby Bath, and blows in and out of the inn from time to time, though not often enough to suit some of their longtime guests, says Haley. "Her presence is felt."

C ircle of Friends

$\mathcal{W}$ hen it comes to business, who can be
more trustworthy than family? That is
why so many entrepreneurs hire family
members, or start businesses with them.
For clothing designer Kevin Simon, an
added dose of confidence comes in
knowing that when she is busy designing, her mother is handling the sewing
and her siblings are running her shop and managing her business. "I feel
secure having them represent me."

And with family working together, she says, there is a kind of shorthand
spoken, less need for explanation, a deeply shared frame of reference. Mickey
Kelly and Susan Kelly Panian, sisters who started the catalogue company
Whispering Pines, know what the other is feeling and thinking. When the
hours get long, as they inevitably do, and the women get punchy, their jokes
are drawn from childhood. No one else but a sister would quite understand.

Husbands and wives working together in business come to know each
other as never before, seeing sides of one another that are simply out of
view in day-to-day domestic life. When they bring complementary skills to
a business partnership, many couples experience a great sense of satisfaction in working together. The business gives them a shared project, a space
in which to grow together and rewards they can share. On the other hand,
for some couples, the togetherness might prove too great. No spouses who
work together will deny that it can put incredible pressure on a marriage,

and learning how to separate the business from the personal aspects of the relationship is something all husband and wife teams need to work at in order to keep their lives balanced.

What is important, say many entrepreneurs, is not to forget that when family members or good friends help out in a business, it is still business. Everyone should be paid for their time and efforts. Also, other employees who are not relatives or close friends should not feel excluded, or be treated differently.

Running a business can be a lonely endeavor, and finding the right partner can make all the difference. Though conventional wisdom suggests otherwise, and the risks can be great, partnerships with a friend can be highly successful, as long as that friend shares a passion for the same things,

a vision for the company, a commitment to hard work, and comes to the partnership with a set of abilities that complement your own.

Many entrepreneurs meet their future business partners in a work setting. This gives them the opportunity to assess each other's work styles and strengths, as well as their compatibility, before taking the enormous plunge of starting an enterprise together. Since owning one's own business is such a labor of love, the bonds that are formed with coworkers and partners are intense and run deep, sometimes nearly as deep as family.

$\mathcal{I}$t's All in the Details

Don't underestimate how attention to detail can attract customers. As always, the display of your products should reflect the simplicity or extravagance of the shop, but feel free to experiment. Even simple touches— merchandise casually arranged in a pretty basket, a simple shelf carrying a colorful and creative display, a handwritten price tag tied with a ribbon—will draw the eye. Also consider the look of your labels, stickers, gift wrap, even shopping bags—they're all part of the visual image you are trying to create.

PROFILES
IN SUCCESS

Once you start down the road of owning your own business, there is a chance that you will discover the latent possibility that you were born to be hugely successful and to preside over a vast, profitable domain. To expand what may have once been a tiny home-based industry into a multimillion-dollar enterprise takes ambition. It also takes a vision, and a willingness to stay true to it.

A bit of luck helps, but that "luck" can be aided by a keen sense of the marketplace. Leslie Ross's beauty and bath supplies business, The Thymes Limited, caught the beginning of a wave, when people were just starting to incorporate relaxation and luxury into their everyday lives. Mixing potions in her kitchen, Leslie picked up on that trend. Rachel Ashwell, founder of Shabby Chic, also had a vision in tune with the times—in her case, of comfortable, beautiful, easy-to-care for furniture. Patti Upton, the founder of Aromatique, created her first decorative fragrance line simply for fun.

Some women are surprised by their success, but it never comes without hard work.

The Thymes Limited

LESLIE ROSS

~

Leslie Ross, the founder and creator of The Thymes Limited, a multimillion-dollar bath, body care, and home fragrance company in Minneapolis, has an infectious and easy laugh. Perhaps she laughs often because she herself finds her success story so unlikely.

It began in 1983, when Leslie, on the verge of turning 30, started feeling restless at her job selling art at her downtown gallery. This, combined with a vague sense of dissatisfaction with the beauty products that were available in stores, encouraged her to begin "doing chemistry," as she calls it, in her kitchen. It turned out to be more alchemy than chemistry.

At the time, she thought she was merely amusing herself, mixing homemade bath soaps out of household items like baking soda, Borax, and essential oils; boiling and distilling flowers to make sweet-scented water; and creating whatever other concoctions salved her curious and enterprising mind. When an

experiment paid off, and she created something fragrant and beautiful, she felt an inordinate pride in the fact that she had made something practically out of nothing. "I felt like it was a much more interesting thing to do than sell artwork," she says. And so she

just kept on making things.

Using about $1,500 worth of savings and the business knowledge she had gained running her gallery, Leslie converted the former gallery space into a shelf-filled showroom. Here, she displayed her bath salts (creatively packaged in Chinese takeout containers), potpourri, herbal wreaths, sachets, and herb vinegars, all in handmade giftwrap. She sent invitations to a sale to everyone who had bought art from her. "I thought they were all humoring me," she says, when her clients turned out in droves to see what Leslie was up to. "It all sold."

A couple more successful sales and Leslie attracted a manufacturers' representative, who suggested that she put together a wholesale list, set of samples, and prices. The

end result was a bitter disappointment—the rep decided she was not interested. "I threw myself on the couch and cried," says Leslie. All cried out, she picked herself up, washed her face, collected her samples, and went to a local shopping area to see if she could sell them herself. That afternoon was another turning point, for many of the merchants bought her wares. From that moment on, Leslie had to take herself seriously as a businessperson.

The high-end and organic beauty products field has become far more competitive than when Leslie first started, and she has had to work hard at continuing to develop

her lines. She has never stopped working on her craft and on her packaging, favoring pretty Japanese patterns. Her packages for items such as cleansing oatmeal grains, exfoliating sea herb soap, and scented candles often have lives long after they are emptied.

As her business grew, Leslie hired a friend as company president, in part to offset her own weaknesses. "I'm more conceptual," she says. "I needed someone who was systematic and good at managing people." There would in time be many more people to manage. Today, The Thymes Limited has 85 employees and numerous departments, including graphics, research and development, sales, and marketing.

Leslie has never lost her taste for alchemy and experimentation, as well as her appreciation for the quiet moments in life that her products are designed to enhance. "Bathing can be a time of reflection, a recollection of the day's events or a preparation for a day of real accomplishment. Rather than focusing on who we are, it's a time that can reveal who we might become." Mixing things in her kitchen, Leslie never imagined becoming the businesswoman she is today.

Habersham Plantation

JOYCE EDDY

~

Joyce Eddy's tale of how she began her wholesale furniture empire, Habersham Plantation, in North Carolina in 1972 is a harrowing and extraordinary odyssey during which both her tenacity, and, she stresses, her faith were indispensable.

Born during the Depression and raised on an Ohio farm, Joyce learned early about hard work and self-reliance. Adulthood brought this farm-bred woman to Georgia where, as a single mother, she inherited a friend's antique "junk" shop above an old laundry in a small town. Serendipitously situated on a tourist route between Florida and the Great Smoky Mountains, the store drew collectors and, in those days, "hippies" who, she noticed, often asked whether she had any primitive, country-style antiques to sell. Endowed with some wood-

working and craft skills, Joyce started to make some of the items they requested, like old

farm tables and jelly cupboards. In the process, she discovered what she calls "magic

stain," a combination of roof cement and mineral spirits that gave the white ponderosa

pine she often worked with a beautiful color.

She began to fashion purses out of cigar boxes, and unusual towel racks and can-

dlestick holders from a whole raft of industrial spools she rescued from the garbage

heap. To her delight and growing confi-

dence, these items and her furniture started

selling briskly. But Joyce soon faced a twin

catastrophe when first her shop, and a short

while later her home, caught fire. No lives

were lost, but precious uninsured antiques,

materials, and keepsakes perished.

With no choice other than to press on,

Joyce took up residence in what remained of her shop and kept making and selling things.

Her oldest son joined the business and their luck improved when a store in Gatlinburg,

Tennessee, offered to sell the furniture they were making. The store even gave Joyce a small advance to get her going. The result was exposure and enough money to expand and hire skilled local craftsmen. Joyce had always admired the way Ethan Allen marketed its furniture, and based on that idea, she opened up galleries to

"I've always had a lot of crazy ideas."

show her furniture the way she thought it should be displayed. In Atlanta, she opened a shop called The Country Store, with furniture, quilts, place mats, pewter pieces, and teddy bears.

Once the look was established, Joyce concentrated on designing and manufacturing furniture—under the name Habersham Plantation—and trying to keep her business healthy during recessionary periods. Along the way she learned how to assess when the

marketplace was ready for new ideas so that the Habersham line could expand. Six years

ago, she was struck with the idea of applying fine arts painting to furniture: trompe l'oeil

designs, copies of Matisse and Renoir paintings, landscapes, and botanical themes. "I

just thought people were bored with the furniture out there," she said. "I've always had

a lot of crazy ideas." This "crazy idea" became a signature look for her furniture.

Today, Habersham Plantation employs 125 people, including 50 artists, and its

furniture is sold in five countries. Joyce's son is president of the company and another

reason for its success. Joyce has experienced lessons as well as triumphs along the way,

including an award as Georgia's best small

business owner in 1984, and a meeting with

then President Reagan. But Joyce has tried

not to let her success get to her head. "We

made every mistake along the way," she says.

Her advice: "Always know your costs. Don't

always listen to so-called experts. Stay

humble and nervous."

Giving Back

Generosity and smart business practices may not be associated in
everyone's mind, but for a great many
successful enterprises, getting involved
in the surrounding community—and
in charitable causes and events—is
a twofold blessing: good for the soul
and good, perhaps in unexpected ways,
for the bottom line. The little secret about giving, as any truly charitable
person will tell you, is that the giver reaps almost as much reward as
the one who receives.

Marlene Harris's antiques business was essentially launched after she
donated an antique button to a charitable auction, which happened to be
attended by an important department store representative who
approached her as a result. This contact led to a lucrative years-long
business relationship and sold her on the importance of giving back some
of the rewards, financial and otherwise, that arise from running a business.
Absent such direct benefits, donations of your wares or services to
charity, from a PTA fund-raiser to an auction for cancer research, raise
the profile of your company, earn it friends and supporters, and give it the
kind of exposure and image that no amount of advertising can buy.

Gaye Parise, owner of The Fire House on Church Street, a shop in
New Milford, Connecticut, that carries an eclectic selection of home furnishings, antiques, and clothing, uses her influence as a successful

businesswoman to try to affect change in her town, where she is actively involved in local environmental causes.

A mark of true success is the desire to give back, since anyone who becomes very successful in business knows they owe a debt of gratitude. Amidst all the making, selling, managing, and hopefully reaping profit, there is a need for balance. Elizabeth Terry, the Savannah chef and restaurateur, regularly donates her wonderful food to charitable events and dinners to raise money for worthy causes, and to the less fortunate living in homeless shelters.

Lindy Phelps and Beryl Hiatt, the owners of Tricoter, have begun a couple of programs which offer free knitting lessons to cancer survivors in local hospitals, a program that Lindy says has gained incredible support from the medical community. This encouraged them to start a program that offered customers a 30 percent discount on yarn to knit hats for women who had lost hair during chemotherapy treatments.

Trina Summins also involves her customers in charity with the "Birthday Club" program at Through the Looking Glass, her children's clothing store in Atlanta. Children in the club receive a free gift, a 10 per-

cent discount on store items, and proceeds from the items purchased are donated to the Atlanta Children's Shelter in the birthday child's name. The New York City–based interior designer Charlotte Moss encourages her employees to serve on junior committees of charities of their own choosing, and sits on several boards herself. "It's the essential cycle," she says. "You work hard, and earn a good living. Then you have to give back. Life is not just a commercial adventure."

The Homestead

CAROL BOLTON

~

Carol Bolton does not mind that many of the visitors who come to her and her husband's six shops in historic Fredericksburg, Texas, just browse, chat, get inspired, have fun, and maybe leave without buying much. Such visits, the word-of-mouth and the positive feelings they generate, are part of what has made the network of interlocking home decorating and furnishings stores she owns with her husband, Tim, such a success.

Carol has a knack for putting things together, a way of resurrecting heirlooms—lace runners, brooches, ribbons, and tablecloths—that might have been stashed away in drawers, a way of making a room tell a story. She might decorate a window frame with vintage postcards, or attach antique gloves to curtains with delicate ribbons. She would never reject a beautiful teapot for

having a chip—it just gives it more character. And she never buys anything for resale that she wouldn't have in her own home. "I'm blessed with a good eye," Carol says. "And being scrappy."

She grew up in the home-furnishings business and had seen first-hand the spirit and energy needed to follow a dream—her father had quit his job when he was in his

"*There were plenty of days when we put up the Gone Fishin' sign . . .*"

fifties to open a store. Carol herself had always been a tireless flea marketer. When she married a man who shared her passions—they spent their honeymoon antiquing—and who had an entrepreneurial bent as well, they moved to Fredericksburg and soon opened their first store. They started small, without so much as a bank loan or much start-up capital, just buying and reselling things that they loved: upholstered furniture, antiques, junky old oil paintings, all of which Carol arranged into charming vignettes. "We used real common objects," she says. "It was the way we put them together."

They did not know it yet, but Fredericksburg was on the verge of becoming a major

weekend destination for Texans and a hub for antiques shoppers. But in the beginning, it was still something of a sleepy little town. "There were plenty of days when we put up the Gone Fishin' sign and closed the shop," says Carol.

The business slowly grew, and before too long, Carol found she wanted to branch out from the bright, cottagey American look they had been celebrating to a darker, European farmhouse look. So they expanded into the dry cleaners shop next door. When she yearned to design garden-themed indoor and outdoor furnishings, she rented space and a courtyard three buildings down and called it Idle Hours. Room No. 5, a store specializing in bed and bath linens and accessories, came next. American Higgeldy Piggeldy, carrying china, old glassware, and table linens, soon followed. Finally, Carol and Tim opened an antiques market called Homestead and Friends, where they host about 25 antiques dealers. What was once a mom-and-pop shop—and is still, to a large extent, a family business, since Carol's mother serves as the office manager and her sister designs the bed linens—has swelled to 60 employees, including craftsmen and designers. In 1997, Carol branched out yet again, designing a line of old-looking new furniture for E. J. Victor, the maker of prestigious traditional furnishings.

"Our business is living proof that if you do it, a little at a time, if you have a unique inventory, and do it out of cash flow, you can succeed," says Carol, who stresses that they

"Our business is living proof . . .
that you can succeed."

were very careful to stay out of debt. "You will make mistakes, but when you do, you just pick yourself up and dust yourself off."

The partnership with her husband is ideal, says Carol, since he is able to make quick and cool-headed business decisions, while she sometimes has trouble divorcing herself emotionally from the business. "For me, it's like our child," she says. A few

years ago, Carol had a baby, and these days she does not mind the store every day as she used to, although when she does, her son comes along.

Shabby Chic

RACHEL ASHWELL

~

Who says just because you have small, spill-prone children that you can't have a lovely house, filled with airy, white furniture, big and soft and enveloping as clouds? Certainly not Rachel Ashwell, and certainly not the empire her comfy slipcovered sofa spawned, Shabby Chic. It may seem a contradiction in terms, but style, on the one hand, and livability, on the other, are what this England-born, southern California-dwelling daughter of a rare-book dealer and restorer of antique dolls is all about.

Like many successful businesswomen, Rachel's vision comes out of her singular background, followed by her insight that the challenges she faced decorating her home while raising two young children could not be unique to her. Her English childhood permanently imbued her with an

eclectic decorating esthetic. It was there that she had her first humble foray into business, a booth at a London flea market where she sold knickknacks and jewelry at the age of 13. When she was older, she moved to Los Angeles to pursue a career as a wardrobe stylist for commercials. She fell in love with the climate and with a native, got married, and decided to stay.

Then came the kids, Lily and Jake, and along with them, the inspiration to fill her home with oversized furniture, covered in wonderful, white—and washable—slipcovers. When friends wanted replicas, she saw her opportunity, and in 1989, she opened the first Shabby Chic store, in Santa Monica. The winning formula caught on from the start, and her shop was soon frequented by celebrities, among others. In the next four years, Rachel opened three more Shabby Chic stores with a partner, Dara Buck, in Chicago, San Francisco, and New York City. Slipcovered furniture was now a nationwide home-furnishing trend, and Shabby Chic spawned imitators; the Los Angeles Times even credited the company with revitalizing the entire Southern California home-furnishings industry.

The partnership between the two women ended, and the business was divided with Rachel retaining control of the Santa Monica and Chicago stores. With the break-up came some painful lessons on the nature of partnership, but Rachel has few regrets. "I knew

nothing about business when I started. Had I known a lot, I might not have taken the risks I took," she says. "Some lessons have been more expensive than others, but as much as some have exhausted me, they've also helped me be a more soulful, creative, and intelligent designer."

Her business, meanwhile, continued to grow and evolve. Its next move was into the wholesale marketplace, first with Shabby Chic Fabrics and then Shabby Chic Home, a line of upscale bedding. One of the biggest hits was Rachel's innovative "T-shirt Sheets," a successful blend of style, simplicity, and comfort. The evolution into bed linens, Rachel swears, had nothing

"Some lessons have been more expensive than others."

to do with cold analysis of the marketplace; rather, she says, "I had a heartfelt passion for bedding." Her passions paid off in another venture as well, as Rachel set them down in two books, the latest of which is called *Rachel Ashwell's Shabby Chic Treasure Hunting and Decorating Guide.*

Rachel now presides over a business that exceeds her wildest dreams. One of the trade-offs of having a multimillion-dollar business, she says, is the acknowledgment that she can no longer control every tiny detail. "Things aren't always going to be perfect," she admits. "It's a hard marriage to be a creative person

and run a company." Finding the right people is essential, she says, and so is letting people do what they are hired to do. "Your team is what makes it fun."

To keep connected to her creative side, Rachel still occasionally wanders through flea markets. "I don't want to lose touch with what inspired me," she says. She also

makes time for her other sources of inspiration, Lily and Jake. "You have to have a balance. As exciting as work is, and as hopefully profitable, it can be all-consuming. You need a life outside of work. You need other things to fall back on."

Old Chatham Sheepherding Inn

NANCY CLARK

~

Nancy Clark, a gifted watercolorist and interior designer, and her husband,

Tom, a partner in a successful Greenwich, Connecticut, investment firm,

had long shared an agrarian impulse. For Tom, it reached back to his child-

hood, when he won a prize at a county fair for three lambs he had raised.

When the couple found a large piece of property in Old Chatham, New

York, in 1993, they could not resist it. They bought the land and the large

Georgian-style mansion (on the National·Register of Historic Places) that

sat on it from the estate of Shaker collector John S. Williams, built barns,

erected fences, and acquired a flock of 150 sheep.

Just five years later, they were running a thriving enterprise on the property, a 13-room antiques-filled inn and an award-winning restaurant frequently cited in the best travel and culinary magazines, a creamery, a farm that now boasts 1,500 sheep, and a store that sells the products the sheep yield—wool, fleece, lamb meat, delicious cheeses and yogurts—goods that will soon be available on the Internet as well. The development of the business, says Nancy, has followed its own undeniable logic. "We started out with the sheep," she says. "Once you have the sheep, you have to shear them, and you have the dairy and meat business. Then, because we opened the inn and the restaurant, we used the products there."

To get the Old Chatham Sheepherding Company Inn up and running in just

five years took the combined energy and talent of the Clarks, and a large investment made possible by Tom's success in finance. Without such resources, Nancy says, the business would have evolved a lot slower. Nancy personally oversaw the renovation and decoration of the inn, and though there is a large staff,

including department heads with considerable responsibility, she is not above scrubbing a toilet if needed, or picking up cigarette butts that have landed on the rolling 500-acre property.

What the Clarks did not have, prior to opening the inn, was experience in the hospitality business. "The whole thing is based on our

"We enjoy it and we get great feedback."

wanting to do things of quality," says Nancy. "We didn't have any experience, but we had traveled, and we knew what we liked." The restaurant, which seats 48 people, is a huge enterprise unto itself. Executive Chef Melissa Kelly, known for her innovative regional cooking, draws much of her inspiration from the farm and its fresh ingredients. "Sheep's milk is richer than cow's milk but lighter than heavy cream," she points out. "So it makes a fine substitute in any recipe that calls for cream. Desserts like crème caramel turn out so light that you can treat yourself even after a hearty entree—my roasted duck, for instance." In the summer, guests can dine outdoors, under a canopy of stars.

The inn and restaurant are located in the middle of nowhere, says Nancy, 35 miles from Albany, not far from the Berkshire Mountains. "At night, it's absolutely black here," she says. Since they were off the main tourist track, initially the Clarks did a lot of advertising, nationally and locally. The high quality and reasonable prices of the inn and restaurant helped to build a loyal following, as did glowing reviews in travel guides. It is the organization as a whole, with all its different elements, that makes the entire enterprise so successful. "Every week, we're doing much better," says Nancy. "We enjoy it, and we get great feedback."

D'Ivy

Avery Green named her company, D'Ivy, after her children, son Damen and daughter Ivy. Children are also the inspiration for her home-based business. Avery hand-crochets baby hats, boots, and sweaters, and adorns them with ribbons, rosettes, and pearl-and-bead clusters. She sells her precious items to retail stores in California and also sells directly to customers who call her with a special request.

Aromatique

Patti Upton

~

Some businesses and businesswomen seem to operate under a charm from the very beginning. Just for fun, one Christmas in the early eighties, Patti Upton arranged a mixture of acorns, pine cones, and hickory nuts native to the foothills of the Ozark Mountains in Arkansas, where she lived; added essential oils and the fragrances of spices like cinnamon; and dubbed her creation The Smell of Christmas. A friend with a gift shop offered to carry the item, and enthralled customers made The Smell of Christmas an instant holiday tradition in the area. Patti could not keep up

with the demand from local shop owners, and had to hire a few employees to help her

whip up the fragrant batches. When spring came around, the shops begged Patti to

create something else for that season. Patti protested that "you can't catch lightning

in a jug twice," but she created The Smell of Spring. It had magic too.

So without ever planning to start a busi-

ness, Patti, a stylish society woman with a

background in fashion, began to envision a

whole new industry: decorative fragrance. It

differs from potpourri in that it combines

visual elements with fragrance, is packaged

differently, is made with large botanicals, and

is scented with evocative essential oils and spices that permeate a room. Soon, Patti

developed other products for a line called The Aromatique Bath, which offers

personal bath items, gift containers, baskets, and candles. That was just the beginning.

Today, the extensive Aromatique line—which includes everything from room spray and

bath oils to candles—is carried in stores throughout North America and in more than

40 foreign countries. The company has long had an office and warehouse in England,

and has recently opened Aromatique London, a gift gallery near Harrod's in London.

Initially, word of Aromatique's unusual offerings traveled from pleased customer to pleased customer. Write-ups in Arkansas society pages, as much about the Upton's lifestyle as Patti's business, helped spread the word. More and more shops contacted Aromatique to buy its goods. For Patti, the idea was never just to make money, it was about creating scents and beauty better than anyone else. "Our success," she says, "is probably due to the fact that this was not meant to be a business. It just happened."

Planned or not, Patti has proven to be a natural businesswoman. She has managed the expansion of her company wisely. She personally approves each new batch of fragrance that Aromatique develops, and says that quality is more important to her  than increasing sales. She also enforces stringent display policies that limit the number of retailers that can carry her line. All Aromatique products must be located in prime floor space, with a large display of open containers of fragrances. "We could

merchandise our products to everyone who requests them and be a much larger company at this point," Patti admits. "But we are in business to stay." This careful approach has helped the company endure where high-flying, fast-growing imitators and competitors have sacrificed quality and failed.

Aromatique is now a hugely successful company that employs over 400 local residents, a boon to the local economy of which Patti is particularly proud. Patti has always been involved with her community and in charitable activities, and through Aromatique she finds she can do even more. A few years ago, Patti created a product called The Natural State, which helps raise money for The Nature Conservancy.

Patti and her husband, Richard, have also bought a resort, The Red Apple Inn, in a lovely part of Arkansas called Eden Isle, eight miles from Aromatique's headquarters. It was not solely a business decision, but rather the Uptons' effort to preserve a historic site that had fallen upon bad times. "It was our gift to the people of Arkansas," says Patti, "and to ourselves."

A Learning Experience

The only thing worse than making mistakes is failing to learn from them.

Joyce Eddy, who heads the Georgia-based Habersham Plantation, a furniture empire, says she made "every mistake in the book." Yet, she has survived them, as well as some downright bad luck—the destruction of her uninsured store by fire—to become the successful businesswoman she is today. Rachel Ashwell, founder of Shabby Chic, went through some difficult times when a partnership she had forged went sour, but has overcome that hurdle and feels she has learned from the experience.

You will not find a successful entrepreneur anywhere who has not made mistakes: errors in hiring, misjudging the market, expanding too fast or in the wrong direction. What sets the successful businesswoman apart is that she often seems to wear a pair of metaphorical blinders that don't allow her to see failure as a possibility. She will do whatever it takes. The difference between success or failure is not in the quantity of mistakes, it's in how you react to them, how quickly you pick yourself up and dust yourself off.

Though there are some things all businesspeople can do to avoid serious problems—keep scrupulous records, hire a trustworthy and reliable staff—missteps will inevitably occur. Speak to other entrepreneurs for advice, make use of consultants at local small business organizations, and read all the books you can on starting and developing a business. Above all, become accustomed to mistakes. They not only can be survived, they can serve a truly positive purpose.

$\mathscr{B}$usiness Resources

Victoria Magazine

Victoria magazine and the *Friends of Victoria* newsletter regularly feature inspirational articles on women who have turned their hobbies into successful businesses. *Victoria's* website (www.victoriamag.com) offers tips on getting started, chat rooms for female entrepreneurs, and lists of useful business resources (government agencies, private associations, and websites). *Victoria* periodically hosts seminars across the country on "Turning Your Passions into Profits," dedicated to helping women begin their own small businesses. For *Victoria* subscriptions in the U.S. and Canada call (800) 876-8696, from elsewhere call (515) 247-7500. For the *Friends of Victoria* newsletter call (800) 846-4020 or (515) 284-0759.

Books:

Body & Soul: Profits with Principles, by Anita Roddick (New York: Crown, 1991).

The inspirational story of Anita Roddick, businesswoman, environmentalist, and founder of The Body Shop International.

Dive Right In—The Sharks Won't Bite: The Entrepreneurial Woman's Guide to Success, by Jane Wesman (Chicago: Dearborn Financial Publishing, Inc., 1995).

A good overview of the issues of starting a business. This book includes a list of helpful books and organizations.

For Entrepreneurs Only: Success Strategies for Anyone Starting or Growing a Business, by Wilson Harrell (Hawthorne, NJ: Career Press, 1994).

Studies the entrepreneurial mind-set, and includes anecdotes and studies of real businesses.

Growing A Business, by Paul Hawken (New York: Simon & Schuster, 1987).

The author, a founding partner of Smith & Hawken, offers sound advice on entrepreneurship. He covers topics from business plans and partnerships to handling money, developing your business, and customer relations.

Guerrilla Marketing, by Jay Conrad Levinson (Boston: Houghton Mifflin, 1993).

The classic book on marketing defines strategies and provides many low-cost ideas. Also by the same author, *Guerrilla Advertising* (Houghton Mifflin, 1994).

How to Run Your Own Home Business, by Coralee Smith and Tammara Hoffman Wolfgram (Lincolnwood, IL: NTC Publishing Group, 1995).

This covers all aspects of running a business out of the home, including legal considerations for service- and product-based businesses, and spotting trends. Especially useful is the recommended reading list.

How to Start and Run Your Own Retail Business: Expert Advice from a Leading Business Consultant and Entrepreneur, by Irving Burstiner (New York: Carol Publishing Group, 1994).

The author addresses important matters for any retail business—choosing the right field; planning, financing, and designing your store; product control—and provides bibliographic references and an appendix with sample income-tax forms.

Inc. Your Dreams, by Rebecca Maddox (New York: Penguin Books, 1995).

Maddox has a good overview of what it takes to realize your full potential and start your own business.

Our Wildest Dreams: Women Entrepreneurs Making Money, Having Fun, Doing Good, by Joline Godfrey (New York: HarperBusiness, 1992).

Relates the experiences of entrepreneurial women throughout the country, and includes interviews, anecdotes, and advice on both business and personal issues.

The Start-Up Guide: A One-Year Plan for Entrepreneurs, by David H. Bangs (Dover, NH: Upstart Publishing Company, 1994).

This practical guide is for individuals with no formal business training. It provides a realistic time frame for tackling business matters before starting a company.

Steps to Small Business Start-Up: Everything You Need to Know to Turn Your Idea into a Successful Business, by Linda Pinson and Jerry Jinnett (Dover, NH: Upstart Publishing Company, 1993).

A hands-on guide that offers a wealth of information on many important topics, including generating business ideas, choosing names, and doing market research. It includes a glossary, resources for small businesses, and sample worksheets. Also by the authors, *Anatomy of a Business Plan, Keeping the Books,* and *Target Marketing for the Small Business.*

Woman to Woman: Street Smarts for Women Entrepreneurs, by Geraldine A. Larkin (Englewood Cliffs, NJ: Prentice Hall, 1993).

This book provides statistics on women-owned businesses and advice on market research, legal issues, budgeting, writing a business plan, and planning for retirement. It also has a short bibliography of business books and a list of helpful organizations, associations, and on-line database services.

The Woman's Guide to Starting a Business, by Claudia Jessup and Genie Chipps (3rd ed., New York: Henry Holt and Company, Inc., 1991).

A great reference book, practical, thorough, and comprehensive. It covers all aspects of starting a small business. Especially useful is its annotated bibliography and list of organizations and associations.

Working Solo Sourcebook: Essential Resources for Independent Entrepreneurs, by Terri Lonier (New Paltz, NY: Portico Press, 1995).

This wonderful book lists business resources for over 40 different fields. It includes helpful government agencies, books, educational programs, videos, professional associations, and advice on how to use these resources efficiently.

MAGAZINES, PERIODICALS, AND DIRECTORIES:

For back articles dealing with topics specific to your business, check with your local library and consult the *Reader's Guide to Periodical Literature,* which lists articles by subject; for example, "Women Entrepreneurs."

Business Plans Handbook

This is a great resource for entrepreneurs needing guidance on writing a business plan. It is a compilation of actual business plans developed by small businesses throughout North America, and also offers sample plans. It includes a glossary, bibliography, and lists all chapters of Small Business Development Centers.

Consumer Information Catalog
Washington, DC, General Services Administration

This offers a list of federal publications of interest to the consumer and businessperson alike. It includes a listing of business development publications, on such topics as starting and managing a business.

Directory of Conventions

Published annually by *Successful Meetings* magazine, with semiannual supplements to keep it current, this directory provides a nationwide listing of trade shows and conventions. It is an invaluable source for finding trade and gift shows appropriate for your industry.

Entrepreneur Magazine

Keeps the small business up-to-date on current trends and small business issues. They also publish *The Entrepreneur Magazine Small Business Series*, which offers various titles, including *Starting a Home-based Business* and *The Entrepreneurial Woman's Guide to Owning a Business*. Call (800) 421-2300 to order.

Fast Company: How Smart Business Works

This magazine highlights practices of the modern business environment. It includes in-depth reports from the most innovative companies, where the focus is no longer centered around the organization but the individual.

Inc.: The Magazine for Growing Companies

Inc. articles focus on small and medium-size businesses. Features include case studies of successful and unsuccessful business ventures; some articles look at female entrepreneurs.

Small Business Sourcebook

This invaluable, two-volume reference publication points out where to go to learn more about small businesses. For each small-business industry (categories include everything from clothing shops to mail-order businesses), it lists a wide variety of information sources, including publications, government and private associations and organizations, start-up information, and trade shows. This is published by Gale Research, Inc. of Detroit.

Trade Show & Convention Guide

This annual publication lists trade shows and conventions around the country. It is published by Billboard Publication Inc. of New York.

ASSOCIATIONS AND ORGANIZATIONS:

The following organizations are invaluable resources for women who would like to start or already have an established business. They offer general, financial, and legal advice, as well as workshops, seminars, mentor programs, information on trade shows and conventions, and networking opportunities. The national headquarters are listed; they can be contacted for a chapter in your area.

American Association of Home-Based Businesses

PO Box 10023
Rockville, MD 20849
(202) 310-3130

This offers networking information for home-based entrepreneurs, and literature on starting a home-based business.

American Booksellers Association (ABA)

828 South Broadway
Tarrytown, NY 10591
(914) 591-2665
www.bookweb.org

ABA is the trade association of independent bookstores. It offers retail aid and publications, as well as many on-line services for members. ABA also provides advice to those in the planning stages of opening a bookstore.

American Business Women's Association (ABWA)

9100 Ward Parkway
PO Box 8728
Kansas City, MO 64114
(816) 361-6621
www.abwahq.org

ABWA has 1,500 chapters nationwide, and offers networking opportunities and information on the latest business trends, continuing education credits, distant-learning certificate programs, and regional and national conferences led by professional speakers and educators from many industries. They also have a range of books, learning tools, and pre-packaged educational programs.

American Craft Council (ACC)

72 Spring Street, 6th Floor
New York, NY 10012
(212) 274-0630

ACC is a national, nonprofit, educational organization for craftspeople. It produces a bimonthly magazine, *American Craft*, organizes annual craft shows around the United States, and offers workshops and seminars for professional craftspeople. The ACC also has a library on 20th-century craft where research staff can assist by mail, e-mail, or telephone with research efforts. The ACC produces many useful research guides, such as *The Business of Craft* and *Careers in Craft*, available free by contacting the library.

American Woman's Economic Development Corporation (AWED)
71 Vanderbilt Avenue, Suite 320
New York, NY 10169
(212) 692-9100/(800) 222-AWED
www.womenconnect.com/awed

AWED offers networking events, training programs on starting your own business and growing an existing one, and entrepreneurial workshops. AWED's faculty, comprised of experienced entrepreneurs and business executives, also provides one-on-one counseling on specific topics such as accounting, marketing, advertising, business law, and business development.

Association of Small Business Development Centers (SBDC)
1050 17th Street NW, Suite 810
Washington, DC 20036
(202) 887-5599

SBDC centers are located throughout the United States, Puerto Rico, and the U.S. Virgin Islands, and are especially useful in developing business plans and providing general start-up information. They are sponsored by the Small Business Administration.

Canadian Association of Women Executives & Entrepreneurs (CAWEE)
2175 Sheppard Avenue East, Suite 310
North York, Ontario M2J 1W8
Canada
(416) 756-0000

CAWEE provides assistance for both female entrepreneurs and executives. It offers monthly events, including workshops, conferences, and speakers. CAWEE meets with other national and international business-women's groups, and holds annual trade shows, including ones designed to help women conduct business globally.

Co-op America
1612 K Street NW, Suite 600
Washington, DC 20006
(202) 872-5307/(800) 424-2667
www.coopamerica.org

This organization provides economic strategies for creating greater social and environmental responsibility, and publishes *National Green Pages*, which provides excellent marketing exposure for small, environmentally friendly businesses.

Council of Better Business Bureaus, Inc. (BBB)
4200 Wilson Boulevard, Suite 800
Arlington, VA 22203
(703) 276-0100
www.bbb.org

BBB acts as a liaison between consumers and businesses and offers advice on improving communication between the two.

Direct Mail Association (DMA)
1120 Avenue of the Americas, 13th Floor
New York, NY 10036
(212) 768-7277

DMA offers services and networking opportunities to traditional mail-order companies and those involved in interactive media. DMA offers conferences, a library and resource center, professional development and training seminars, and DMA publications that keep members up-to-date on legislative issues effecting the industry.

The Entrepreneurship Institute
3592 Corporate Drive, Suite 101
Columbus, OH 43231
(614) 895-1153
www.tei.net/tei

TEI chapters are dedicated to providing opportunities for small and mid-market businesses to grow their companies. Advisory boards are comprised of successful business owners, bankers, accountants, business attorneys, and investors, and offer educational and networking programs.

National Association of the Self-Employed
2121 Precinct Line Road
Hurst, TX 76054
(800) 232-NASE

This association provides the self-employed with group health benefits, tax information, and updates on relevant legislative issues. It also offers members discounts on services provided by large business firms, computer training, and useful publications.

National Association of Women Business Owners
(NAWBO)
1377 K Street NW
Washington, DC 20005
(202) 638-5322
www.nawbo.org

NAWBO represents the interests of women entrepreneurs in all types of businesses. There are currently over 60 chapters, and the organization is affiliated with Les Femmes Chefs d'Entreprises Mondiales (World Association of Women Entrepreneurs). Their on-line services include information on business magazines, business and industry resources, and international links to associations like the Canadian Women's Business Network and Women-Connect-Asia.

National Chamber of Commerce for Women
10 Waterside Place, Suite 6H
New York, NY 10010
(212) 685-3454

The chamber is a great source for business and employment data. It offers surveys of funding sources, examines financing and operations of women-owned ventures, and offers business plans and industry surveys.

National Education Center
for Women in Business (NECWB)
Seton Hill College
Seton Hill Drive
Greensburg, PA 15602-1599
(800) 632-9248/(412) 830-4625
www.necwb.setonhill.edu

NECWB's mission is to enable the economic self-sufficiency of women through advocacy and educational initiatives in entrepreneurship. It offers courses and sponsors Strategy 2000, a one-day

seminar presented throughout the country that assists women in starting and growing their own businesses. Ongoing information is provided in its newsletter, *The NECWB Source*, and its website.

National Federation of Black
Women Business Owners (NFBWBO)
1500 Massachusetts Avenue NW, Suite 22
Washington, DC 20005
(202) 833-3450

NFBWBO provides networking, educational, and financial guidance to members, and offers education and training through seminars, conferences, trade fairs, and discussions with experts from federal and private-sector corporations. Its workshops focus on business development and access to capital and credit.

National Federation of Independent Businesses
(NFIB)
600 Maryland Avenue SW, Suite 700
Washington, DC 20024
(202) 554-9000
www.nfibonline.com

NFIB is an advocacy organization founded to give small and independent businesses a voice in governmental decision-making. The NFIB website offers information on IRS codes, medical savings accounts, and small business news.

National Foundation for
Women Business Owners (NFWBO)
1100 Wayne Avenue, Suite 830
Silver Spring, MD 20910
(301) 495-4975
www.nfwbo.org

NFWBO is a research and leadership-training foundation that offers a comprehensive source of information and statistics on women business owners and their businesses.

RoundTable for Women in Foodservice (RWF)
1372 La Colina Drive #B
Tustin, CA 92780
(714) 838-2749
www.rwf.org

RWF is a national foodservice industry trade association for female operators, suppliers, and service professionals, committed to developing women's careers in the food industry through education and networking. It was founded to represent the ascending role of women in professional positions within the foodservice industry.

Small Business Administration (SBA)
409 3rd Street SW, 4th Floor
Washington, DC 20416
(800) 827-5722
www.sba.gov

SBA is an invaluable organization that provides vast amounts of information: how to seek capital, how to comply with tax codes, where to find advice, how to develop your product, how to manage growth. SBA publishes *The Small Business Resource Guide*, which lists sources of assistance for small businesses in the federal, state, and private sectors. Call the Small Business Answer Desk at the number listed above for general inquiries about SBA services and resources from federal, state, and local government agencies.

Office of Women's Business Ownership (OWBO)
(202) 205-6673
www.owbo.sba.gov

OWBO, a division of SBA, offers specific help for women business owners, and has a new Online Women's Business Center at www.onlinewbc.org. This is a free, interactive, state-of-the-art Internet website for beginning and established women business owners.

Small Business Center
Fashion Institute of Technology
227 W. 27th Street, Room C-110
New York, NY 10001
(212) 217-7250
www.fitnyc.edu

FIT's Small Business Training Program offers classes in financing, marketing, money management, business law, and press and publicity. FIT also offers the Creative Enterprise Ownership Certificate Program, which focuses on business training for artists, designers, and fashion-industry professionals, and the Women Business Owners Program, a 6-week intensive workshop that helps women with established businesses to expand and improve the profitability of their enterprises.

U.S. Chamber of Commerce
1615 H Street, NW
Washington, DC 20062
(202) 659-6000
www.uschamber.org

The U.S. Chamber of Commerce works with local and state chambers and represents national business interests to the federal government. It also publishes many useful guides, including *The Small Business Resource Guide* and *The Small Business Financial Resource Guide*. Local chambers are especially useful for small businesses, and run programs on small business start-up and development, counsel on small business problems, and provide start-up assistance, lending, and equity capital programs.

Women Chefs & Restaurateurs
304 W. Liberty Street, Suite 201
Louisville, KY 40202
(502) 581-0300
www.wcr@HQTRS.com

WCR promotes the education and advancement of women in the restaurant industry, from executive chefs to culinary students and restaurant owners, and the betterment of the industry as a whole. It is an advocate for a healthier, safer restaurant industry and actively promotes workplace flexibility, including job sharing and child care.

Women's World Banking (WWB)
8 W. 40th Street, 10th Floor
New York, NY 10018
(212) 768-8513

An international organization that offers business development services to help entrepreneurs. WWB produces and disseminates research, publications, and videos on women in business.

$\mathscr{B}$usiness Directory

Ambrosia's Garden
1204 E. Atlantic Avenue
Delray Beach, FL 33483
(561) 272-9860
pages 148 (photo), 156-160

An Egg by Jane
PO Box 2605
Westport, CT 06880
(203) 866-1032
www.janepollak.com
page 105

Archivia Books
944 Madison Avenue
New York, NY 10021
(212) 439-9194
pages 88-91

Aromatique, Inc.
PO Box 1500
Heber Springs, AR 72543
(501) 362-7511
pages 74, 206-210

Bell'occhio
8 Brady Street
San Francisco, CA 01907
(415) 864-4048
www.bellocchio.com
Back jacket, top left;
pages 34, 173 (photo)

Bonne Bouche
Catering
PO Box 1573
Capitola, CA 95010
(408) 479-9637
pages 56-59

Bravura
343 Vermont Street
San Francisco, CA 94103
(415) 474-9092
pages 40-43

Buckingham Mercantile
466 South Coast
   Highway 101
Encinitas, CA 92024
(760) 436-7666
pages 36-39

Bungalow Antiques &
Decorations
4 Sconset Square
Westport, CT 06880
(203) 227-4406
page 25 (photo)

Bunnies by the Bay
2916 Commercial Avenue,
   Suite B266
Anacortes, WA 98221
(800) 342-4690
page 53 (photo)

Charlotte Moss
& Company
16 E. 65th Street
New York, NY 10021
(212) 772-6244
pages 75, 163, 187

Conni Cross
Garden Design
Box 730
Cutchogue, NY 11935
(516) 734-6874
pages 60-63, 162 (photo), 163

Cornelia Powell
271-B E. Paces Ferry Road
Atlanta, GA 30305
(404) 365-8511
www.corneliapowell.com
pages 92-97

Cucina
256 Fifth Avenue
Brooklyn, NY 11215
(718) 230-0711
page 117 (photo)

Debby DuBay
Limoges Antiques
20 Post Office Avenue
Andover, MA 01810
(978) 470-8773
pages 98-101, 145, 162

D'Ivy
4510 Murietta Avenue, #5
Sherman Oaks, CA 91423
(818) 990-2051
page 205

The Elegant Earth
1907 Cahaba Road
Birmingham, AL 35223
(800) 242-7758
page 52 (photo)

Elizabeth on 37th
105 E. 37th Street
Savannah, GA 31401
(912) 236-5547
www.elizabethon37th.com
pages 51, 80-83, 187

Erbe
196 Prince Street
New York, NY 10013
(212) 966-1445/
(800) 432-ERBE
page 34

Erna's Elderberry House
48688 Victoria Lane
Oakhurst, CA
(209) 683-6860
page 171 (photo)

The Fire House on Church Street
19 Church Street
New Milford, CT 06776
(860) 355-2790
page 186

Foxglove Farm
6741 224th Street
Langley, BC V3A 6H4
Canada
(604) 888-4140
page 163

Garden Memories
67 S. California Street
Ventura, CA 93001
(805) 641-1070
page 170 (photo)

Garlands
545 Beachland Boulevard
Vero Beach, FL 32963
(561) 234-2908
pages 148, 156-160

Grandmother's Buttons
PO Box 1689
St. Francisville, LA 70775
(504) 635-4107
Front jacket, bottom left

Grasmere
40 Maple Avenue
Barrington, RI 02806
(401) 247-2789
Front jacket, bottom right;
pages 126-129

The Grey Havens Inn
PO Box 308
Georgetown Island,
ME 04548
(207) 371-2616
www.greyhavens.com
pages 164-169

Habersham Plantation
171 Collier Road
Toccoa, Georgia 30577
(800) 241-0716
www.habershamplantation.com
pages 65, 74, 182-185, 211

Hannah's Treasures
1103 Seventh Street
Harlan, IA 51537
(712) 755-3173
www.hannahstreaures.com
page 129

Homestead
223 E. Main Street
Fredericksburg, TX 78624
(830) 997-5551
Back jacket, bottom right;
pages 145, 188-193

Joyce Ames Lampshades
New York, NY
(212) 799-8995
pages 112-114

Kevin Simon Clothing
1358 Abbot Kinney
   Boulevard
Venice, CA 90291
(310) 392-4630
Front jacket, top right;
pages 14-19, 170

Lark Roderigues
73 W. Passage Drive
Portsmouth, RI 02871
(401) 683-5298
pages 20-22

Lilac Bow Yoke
1812 6th Street, Building B
Berkeley, CA 94710
(510) 548-5448
page 18

Lisa Parks Knits
244 E. Maple Road
Birmingham, MI 48009
(248) 332-1313
page 52 (photo)

Lola Millinery
New York, NY
(212) 279-9093
Front jacket, top left;
page 147 (photo)

Louise Green Millinery Company
1616 Cotner Avenue
Los Angeles, CA 90025
(310) 479-1881
pages 48-50, 75

Marlene Harris Collection
238½ Freeport Road
Blawnox, PA 15238
(412) 828-1245
pages 65, 102-105, 186

Marston House
PO Box 517
Wiscasset, ME 04587
(207) 882-6010
pages 138, 142-144

Mary Nell's
270 Riverside Drive
New York, NY 10025
(212) 865-8370
pages 20-23

Nancy Koltes Fine Linens
New York, NY
(212) 995-9050
pages 106-108

Nancy's Wines for Food
313 Columbus Avenue
New York, NY 10023
(212) 877-4040
page 83

Old Chatham Sheepherding Inn
99 Shaker Museum Road
Old Chatham, NY 12136
(518) 794-9774
www.oldsheepinn.com
pages 75, 200-205

Patina Millinery
1679 N. Dillon Street
Los Angeles, CA 90026
(323) 931-6931
page 147 (photo)

Patticakes
1900 N. Allen Avenue
Altadena, CA 91001
(818) 794-1128
page 34

Paula Gins Antique Linens
7233 S. Sundown Circle
Littleton, CO 80120
(303) 734-9095
pages 107, 110-111

Pendragon, Ink
27 Prospect Street
Whitinsville, MA 01588
(508) 234-6843
page 34

The Pillowmaker
New York, NY
(800) 611-5722
www.thepillowmaker.com
page 111

Pink Rose Pastry Shop
630 S. Fourth Street
Philadelphia, PA 19147
(215) 592-9321
Back jacket, bottom left; pages 66-69

Pooter Olooms
339 State Street
Harbor Springs, MI 49740
(616) 526-6101
Back case image, page 35

Potluck Studios
23 Main Street
Accord, NY 12404
(914) 626-2300
Back jacket, top right; pages 65 (photo), 75, 120-124, 145

Potted Gardens
27 Bedford Street
New York, NY 10014
(212) 255-4797
pages 70-74

Red Apple Inn
1000 Country Club Road
Heber Springs, AK 72543
(800) RED-APPLE
pages 53 (photo), 210

Reiko M.
734 S. Washington
Royal Oak, MI 48067
(248) 543-5433
pages 53 (photo), 171 (bottom photo)

Renaissance Buttons
826 W. Armitage Avenue
Chicago, IL 60614
(773) 883-9508
www.renaissancebuttons.com
page 52 (photo)

Rosa Rugosa
10 Straight Wharf
Nantucket, MA 02554
(508) 228-5597
pages 148 (photo), 156-160

Shabby Chic
6365 Arizona Circle
Los Angeles, CA 90045
(800) 876-3226/
(310) 258-0660
pages 51, 75, 194-199, 211

Shale Hill Farm and Herb Garden
134 Hommelville Road
Saugerties, NY 12477
(914) 246-6982
page 65 (photo)

Stonehouse Farm Goods: The Store
544 W. Water Street
Princeton, WI 54968
(888) 382-4500
pages 150-154

Summer Cottage
3573 Larkspur Lane
Carmel, IN 46032
(317) 466-5872
www.summercottage.com
page 124

T Salon
11 E. 20th Street
New York, NY 10003
(212) 358-0506
page 146 (photo)

Tail of the Yak
2632 Ashby Avenue
Berkeley, CA 94705
(510) 841-9891
page 35

Tancredi & Morgen
7174 Carmel Valley Road
Valley Hills Center
Carmel, CA 93923
(408) 625-4477
pages 138-142

Through the Looking Glass
3802 Roswell Road
Atlanta, GA 30342
(404) 231-4007
pages 35, 186 (photo), 187

The Thymes Limited
420 N. Fifth Street
Minneapolis, MN 55401
(612) 338-4471
pages 176-181

Tracy Porter: The Home Collection
N5373 County Road W
Princeton, WI 54968
(920) 295-0142
pages 75, 150-154

Tricoter
3121 E. Madison Street
Seattle, WA 98112
(206) 328-6505
page 187

Vanessa Noel
12 W. 57th Street, Suite 901
New York, NY 10019
(212) 333-7882
pages 30-33

Victory Garden
63 Main Street
East Hampton, NY 11937
(516) 324-7800
pages 53 (photo), 172-3 (photo)

Wells-Ware
PO Box 1596
New York, NY 10025
(888) 90WELLS
www.wellsware.com
pages 44-47

Whispering Pines
43 Ruane Street
Fairfield, CT 06430
(203) 259-5027
www.whispering-pine.com
pages 75, 130-135, 175

White Linen
520 Bedford Road
Pleasantville, NY 10570
(800) 828-0269/
(914) 769-4551
pages 107-110

Wild Child
333 Main Street
Wakefield, RI 02879
(401) 782-8944
www.sprig.net
pages 9, 26-29

Yesteryear Ltd.
8816 Beverly Boulevard
Los Angeles, CA 90048
(310) 278-2008
pages 75-78

$\mathcal{P}$hoto Credits

Index